DECKS

By the Editors of Sunset Books

Deck sections and alternating steps descend gradually from house to yard (also shown on page 35).

Decking, rimmed with brick, echoes lines of pool, invites sunbathing and alfresco dining (also shown on page 23).

Research & Text
Don Vandervort

Coordinating Editor
Deborah Thomas Kramer

Design
Joe di Chiarro

Illustrations
Bill Oetinger

Photographers: Patrick Barta, 31 top, 42 top left, 43 bottom right; **California Redwood Association,** 9 bottom, 10 bottom, 11, 12 bottom, 18 bottom, 24, 29 top left and right, 31 bottom, 36 top, 38 bottom left and right, 39 bottom right, 41 top left and bottom right, 42 bottom right, 43 top left and right; **Glenn Christiansen,** 22 top; **Peter Christiansen,** 13 bottom right, 37 bottom; **Stephen Cridland,** 9 center, 10 top, 15 bottom left, 21, 35 bottom, 39 bottom left, 41 bottom left, 43 bottom left; **Derek Fell,** 5; **David Franzen,** 26; **Jerry Fredrick,** 22 bottom; **Philip Harvey,** 2, 6, 13 top, 15 bottom right, 23 top; **Jack McDowell,** 8 bottom, 12 top, 14 bottom, 18 top, 29 bottom, 30 bottom, 31 center, 34 top, 38 top, 39 top right; **Stephen Marley,** 15 top, 16 top, 17 bottom, 19 top, 20, 23 bottom, 27 top left, top right, and bottom left, 28 top, 30 top, 37 top left, center, and right, 40 top; **Ells Marugg,** 8 top, 9 top, 39 top left, 40 bottom; **Richard Nicol,** 13 bottom left, 17 top, 25 top and bottom, 32, 34 bottom, 36 bottom, 42 top right; **Don Normark,** 28 bottom, 47; **Norman A. Plate,** 1, 16 bottom, 35 top right, 42 bottom left; **David Stubbs,** 14 top; **Tom Wyatt,** 19 bottom, 23 center, 25 center, 27 bottom right, 35 top left, 41 top right, 44, 46.

All Decked Out for Fun

No longer a lifestyle confined to warm, sunny climes, outdoor living is enjoyed by people everywhere. As a result, a deck has become a basic accoutrement of today's home as a stage for summer parties, a place to relax or sunbathe, an alfresco dining room, or a garden floor.

A simple low-level deck can be a rewarding do-it-yourself project. This book presents colorful up-to-minute deck designs, takes you step-by-step through the crucial planning process, and details the construction techniques you'll need to build your own deck. It also explains how to add benches, overheads, and other amenities to outfit your deck for comfort and convenience.

Special thanks go to Rebecca LaBrum for carefully editing the manuscript, to JoAnn Masaoka Van Atta for styling some of the photographs, and to Marianne Lipanovich for scouting some of the photography locations. We also want to thank the California Redwood Association for their invaluable assistance, as well as Golden State Lumber, Brett Simison, David Vandervort, and Western Wood Products Association.

Cover: Planters, seating, and outdoor lighting all contribute to the comfort and enjoyment of this expansive hillside deck. Architect: Curtis Gelotte Architects. Cover design: Susan Bryant. Photography by Richard Nicol. Photo styling by JoAnn Masaoka Van Atta.

Editorial Director, Sunset Books: Kenneth Winchester

Eighth printing September 1994

CONTENTS

THE
OUTDOOR
STAGE

No matter where we live, outdoor living is a time-honored pleasure. We go outdoors to shake off daily stresses, recharge our spirits, and engage in our favorite pastimes—the kids roughhouse, Grandpa relaxes in the shade, and Mom and Dad preside at the barbecue.

It's our love of the outdoors that makes decks so popular. Comfortable, attractive, and adaptable to almost any situation, a deck offers the perfect stage for playing out those wonderful outdoor moments. And decks bring other benefits, too.

■ **A deck increases the usable square footage** of your house for a fraction of the cost of adding rooms.

■ **A deck invites your guests out to enjoy the garden,** saving your home's kitchen, dining room, and entertainment areas from wear and tear. If you add a few extra features, your deck can provide storage, seating, and outdoor work surfaces.

■ **A nondescript house takes on new dimension,** detailing, and line when a deck is added. At poolside or in the garden, a deck can become a dynamic landscape element, a focal point for the whole yard. A series of decks can integrate patios, pools, flower beds, and other landscape features. And a house-attached deck visually enlarges interior rooms by extending the floor line outward.

■ **A well-designed and carefully built deck** enhances your home's value.

Capturing the outdoors for entertaining and enjoyment, large deck unifies house with beautifully landscaped yard. Multiple levels gently flow from main deck to lower deck and then to garden. Landscape architect: Brickman Industries.

A GALLERY OF DECK STYLES

The gallery of decks on the following pages will stimulate your imagination and spark your enthusiasm, helping you create a deck that's just right for your family. You'll discover how others—in many cases professional designers or builders—have tackled the challenge of deck design.

The simple term "deck" covers a wide variety of outdoor structures: modest ground-hugging platforms, spectacular high-level edifices, split-level decks, entry boardwalks, raised poolside surfaces. On the following pages you'll find examples of almost all these types.

Plan views are given for some of the decks pictured here. Though it's unlikely that your site and conditions will correspond exactly to those shown, you may be faced with a similar situation—and the plans and photos may help you decide how best to tackle your project.

Favored for a gradually sloping yard, multilevel deck stays close to the ground, yet offers flat surfaces. Deck's built-in benches and planters funnel foot traffic and serve as low railings. Landscape architect: Ransohoff, Blanchfield & Jones, Inc.

GARDEN FLOORS

Easy-to-make low-level decks that expand your living space

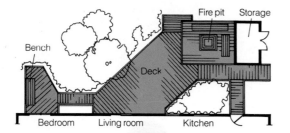

Like a classic boardwalk, rambling series of low-level decks offers space for a range of activities. Raised platform is a barbecue center. Architect: Bennett, Johnson, Slenes & Smith.

Transforming a forgotten backyard corner, low-level deck features built-in benches and planter. Angled edges add visual interest to deck and help soften yard's stark rectangular shape. Landscape architect: Jim Coleman.

Built over an existing patio, handsome deck provides a center for alfresco meals and relaxation. Picnic table and benches match deck; tub is transformed into a table when its wooden lid is in place. Design: Ed Hoiland.

Fronting a sandstone-edged pool, carefully crafted low-level deck adds to enjoyment of secluded, intimate backyard. Landscape architect: Thomas L. Berger Associates.

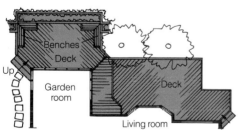

Dense shade in wooded hillside backyard made for poor growing conditions. The solution? Open up space with an 800-square-foot redwood deck, complete with retaining wall and built-in planters. Design: Edward Assa, Ace Custom Decks.

MULTILEVEL DECKS

Multiple levels that break up space, follow land's contours

Stained cedar deck *offers broad landings for easy access. Careful detailing includes matching benches and planter. Landscape architect: John Herbst, Jr.*

Three-level redwood deck *provides an easy transition from house to backyard. Lowest level—three steps up from concrete patio—is a sunning platform; spa deck at second level receives plenty of sun, too. Upper level is shaded by an overhead. Design: L. Dennis Shields, California Contemporary Landscape.*

Redwood decks drop gradually, stepping down 6 feet from house to backyard. Matching railings, benches, and planters visually link levels and guide foot traffic. Homeowners can dine on shaded upper deck, bubble in spa on middle level, or sunbathe on lower level. Design: Picardi Construction.

Four overlapping redwood platforms create graceful terraced deck. Besides providing splashes of color, built-in planters help direct traffic. Guests can sit on perimeter built-in benches or directly on steps. Design: John Matthias.

A stunning design for a natural setting: a series of decks built from lively garden grades of redwood draw house and forested backyard together. Design: Jim Babcock.

HILLSIDE DECKS

Decks that soar over steep sites

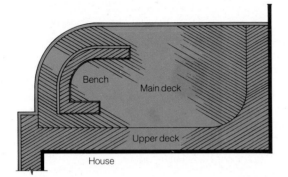

Curved railings and bench echo sweeping wraparound view from this handsome redwood deck. Like many hillside decks, this one required special construction: for piers, engineer drilled down 32 feet to reach stable soil. Design: Gary Marsh.

Enjoy the view from a private box seat: a handsome cantilevered deck floating above a sea of trees. Support is provided by heavy laminated beams extending from house and by steel tension rods reaching from roof beams to deck. Design: James A. Jennings.

Steep hillside lot was reclaimed by adding rectangular deck. Redwood bench masks retaining wall. Landscape architect: David Gibson

Overlooking a panoramic view, curved and comfortable hillside deck invites guests outdoors for dining and relaxation. Design: Gary Marsh.

Finely detailed painted deck integrates hillside home with sloping terrain, providing plenty of usable outdoor space on several levels. Deck, also shown on front cover, was designed at same time as house. Architect: Curtis Gelotte Architects.

ROOFTOP SOLUTIONS

Sometimes it's best to go up, not out

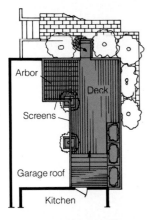

Garage-top deck *expands space for entertaining and helps link indoors with outdoors. Opening off dining room, main part of deck covers an 18-foot-square flat-roofed garage. An extension beneath living room windows ends in a balcony that's curved like top of a grand piano. Architects: Robert Swatt and Bernard Stein.*

Sun or shade? *This rooftop deck gives you a choice: pleasant shade in arbor or direct sun on rest of deck. Plants and cedar screens ensure privacy. Landscape architect: Robert W. Chittock.*

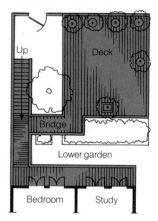

Linked to house by a second-story bridge, converted garage roof offers spacious outdoor living on a tight city lot. Lattice rails are painted to match house trim. Design: Ron Pimentel.

Nestled behind a section of pitched roof over a two-car garage, lattice-railed rooftop deck creates a private retreat at back corner of property. Landscape architect: Thomas L. Berger Associates.

Parking deck perches over a workout room on a steep hillside lot. Like nearly all rooftop decks, this one was designed by qualified professionals. Landscape architect: Royston, Hanamoto, Alley & Abey.

THE DIRECT APPROACH

Bridges and entryways that extend a warm welcome

Bridging a sloping site, redwood entry deck provides a level approach to front door. Lamp posts and bevel-topped railings create a neat and finished look. Architect: Ron Yeo.

Small but effective entry deck joins house to driveway. Nicely detailed railings and planters set tone for this home's front yard landscaping. Landscape architect: John Herbst, Jr.

Enclosed entry deck gradually steps toward house. Choice of materials helps deck blend with house—both deck railings and house walls are covered with same lap siding. Landscape architect: John M. Bernhard.

Key to an effective face-lift, front yard deck turned a small, sunny, but too-public space into an attractive area for outdoor living and entertaining. A new fence encloses remodeled yard. Landscape architect: The Runa Group, Inc.

DECKS FOR SOAKING

When a spa or hot tub is the star attraction

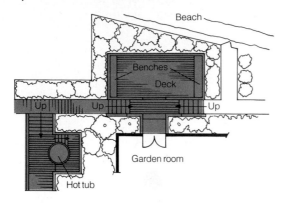

Soaking in a great view, *hot-tub deck is one of two decks at this waterfront setting (see plan at left). Decks have shingled, painted rails that match home's siding and trim. Architect: Bennett, Johnson, Slenes & Smith.*

Thoughtful detailing *of spa deck features decking laid in a diagonal pattern, low benches around spa, and a combination bench/table surrounding a shady tree. Economical, knot-textured garden-grade redwood enhances design. Design: Ken Butler.*

Echoing spa's octagonal shape, *this deck is about 18 inches above water line, providing seating for sunbathers.*

Small steps spiral *around a classic barrel-shaped hot tub. A taper jig and table saw make short work of tapering deck boards, speeding up construction of this minimum-space design. Design: Roger D. Fiske.*

POOLSIDE PLATFORMS

Pool surrounds for fun in the sun

New wooden pool surround *covers a worn and outdated concrete pool deck. To avoid labor and expense of replacing old surface, homeowners simply built a new deck-and-step combination right on top. Architect: CZL Associates.*

Deck meets pool edge perfectly *for a sleek, flush-mounted look. Wraparound bench is functional in more ways than one: sections of its top are hinged, opening up to reveal storage space beneath. Landscape architect: Thomas E. Baak.*

Above-ground pool *on steep hillside is flanked by intricate stained redwood deck. Horizontal trellis around outer perimeter eliminates need for a standard railing. Landscape architect: John Herbst, Jr.*

POOLSIDE PLATFORMS

Generous deck surrounds an unusual pool made from a wine-processing vat. Graduated levels break up expanse and provide plenty of space for seating and potted plants. Design: Rick Morrall.

Corner deck is just the spot for sunbathing. Deck is wedged into hillside, giving narrow yard greater depth. Design: Wimmer, Yamada & Associates.

Step-up deck next to pool and spa provides a stage for entertaining or sunbathing. Combination pipe and solid wood railing allows view, yet offers sense of enclosure. Landscape architect: Royston, Hanamoto, Alley & Abey.

Inventive pool deck crosses over small swimming pool, then zigzags its way around a generous spa where it meets another deck, this one linking spa with a gazebo tucked away in greenery at left. Landscape architect: Woodward Dike.

Poolside redwood deck almost seems to float, thanks to rocks partially embedded in concrete to camouflage piers and footings. More rocks judiciously arranged throughout garden vary yard's overall linear look. Decking on both sides of pool is laid in a parallel pattern, with alternating 2 by 2s and 2 by 6s. Landscape architect: Lang & Wood.

SMALL-SPACE DECKS

Intimate decks that fit your space and your lifestyle

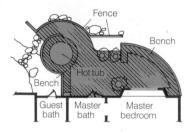

Sculptured curves of tiny privacy deck make the most of an almost unusable hillside backyard. To enjoy both redwood deck and hot tub, owners just step out new bedroom French doors. Design: Gary Marsh.

Tucked into an alcove where two wings of house meet, redwood deck offers ample space for relaxation and outdoor dining. Lattice-work screen contributes to feeling of seclusion and privacy. Design: Decks Unlimited, Inc.

Taking advantage of a lookout point, small bow-shaped deck is detached from house. Lap-sided railings enclose broad benches; on view side, wide-spaced railing allows eye-level enjoyment of panorama when you're seated. Landscape architect: Thomas L. Berger Associates.

Small side yard, once wasted space, became a favorite spot with addition of low-level deck, brick patio, planting beds, and overhead trellis. Landscape architect: Fry + Stone Associates.

Small in size but big on details, this appealing deck provides plenty of easy-care surface area for a small backyard. Lattice-work along base of deck keeps out critters, hides view of substructure. Design: Swanson's Nursery & Landscaping.

OUTDOOR ROOMS

Enclosed spaces for year-round enjoyment

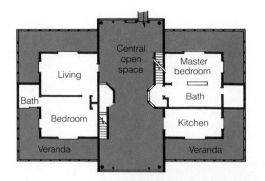

Open beams, rafters, and spaced-lath roofing *cover central outdoor space of this Hawaiian home. As shown in symmetrical first-floor plan (at right), living room, bedrooms, and kitchen are actually surrounded by covered outdoor space. Architect: William Turnbull.*

Japanese garden room (at right) replaced an old concrete patio, providing owners with year-round indoor-outdoor living. On warm days, shojii-like screens (below) slide aside and stack to let in fresh air. Architect: Alan Oshima.

Translucent shojiis and paneling help make this spa a private retreat. Tiny deck steps up and surrounds spa. Design: Keith Wallach.

Small gazebo cantilevers over a rock-edged swimming pool. Open-sided redwood structure, styled to resemble a traditional Japanese teahouse, blends easily with redwood deck beyond. Design: William Churchill. Landscape design: Edwin Simon.

STAND-ALONE STRUCTURES

Wooded retreats and satellite decks for private reflection, lounging, and entertaining

Wedged against a hillside *in backyard, rectangular redwood deck draws attention to garden and gives youngsters a compact play platform. Deck surface is made from 2 by 2s and 2 by 6s laid in concentric squares over a diagonal joist system. Wood retaining wall supports built-in bench. Landscape architect: Lang & Wood.*

Two overlapping semicircles *(10 and 16 feet in diameter) of cedar 2 by 3s float on six pressure-treated poles to make a little island for dining, chatting, and just relaxing. Architect: Jeremy Miller.*

Avoiding the dull slab approach to landscaping, compact redwood deck combines with lawn, shrubs, and concrete aggregate paving to create a dramatic, low-maintenance backyard. Design: Don and Laura Braseco.

Filling up an unused corner, easy-to-build redwood deck surrounds hot tub, offers built-in benches. Design: Larry and Florence Regular.

Shaded and sheltered by trees, scaled-down deck offers a comfortable spot for quiet conversation and informal entertaining. Built-in bench takes the place of a railing. Landscape architect: Thomas E. Baak.

SHAPES & PATTERNS

Creative arrangements that make a design statement

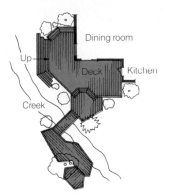

A medley of angles and planes, garden decking bridges a small natural creek and leads to house. Though a deck like this one is a bit more difficult to build than the standard rectangular model, it's well worth the effort. Landscape architect: John Herbst, Jr.

Curving teardrop deck invites you into garden for early-morning coffee and evening conversation. Nestled in a cluster of evergreens, it's just a step away from master bedroom and nearby patio. Design: C.A. and Elva Powell.

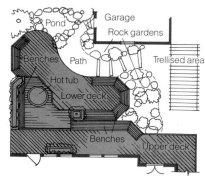

Meandering redwood deck *follows garden contours and plantings, making a fairly small yard seem more spacious. Design: Judith L. Donaghey.*

True elegance— *this deck has it, thanks to concentric squares and herringbone patterns. Screens and an overhead add interest. Landscape architect: Donald G. Boos.*

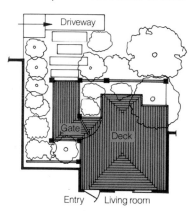

Parquet pattern *transforms what would otherwise be an uninteresting design into a dynamic one. Pattern allows for use of short, cutoff lengths of redwood decking, but requires mitering and generates extra waste from angled cuts. Design: Dettmer Brothers Construction.*

DETAILS: A CLOSER LOOK

Fanciful, classic, utilitarian: what style do you prefer? Though most decks are essentially wooden surfaces, their overall appearance is easily altered with the addition of railings, overheads, stairs, benches, and other amenities.

Of course, details aren't strictly cosmetic—they should be functional, too. Steps carry you from one level to another, railings provide armrests and guard against falls, benches offer welcome seating, and overheads and screens lend shelter. Planters offer greenery and seasonal color; storage compartments help minimize clutter.

On the following pages, we've gathered an assortment of functional and good-looking deck details. When you're choosing a style for your deck, look through this collection for inspiration.

Integral railings, benches, and lighting are all part of this finely detailed view deck. Saw kerfs in post tops and handcrafted deck lights add to effect. Architect: Curtis Gelotte Architects.

STEPS & STAIRS

Getting there is half the fun

Like a stack of nesting boxes, steps lead through wooded garden from one deck level to the next. Mid-level platform is large enough to accommodate a bench. Design: Steve Burris.

Stately stairway drops from deck to lower patio. Railings, a major part of design, are made of clear Western red cedar. Latticework screen masks storage area below stairs. Design: Swanson's Nursery & Landscaping.

Paired railroad tie sections link two decks set at different levels. Ties are virtually indestructible, and their dimensions make it simple to build steps with ideal riser-to-tread ratios. Landscape architect: Michael Painter.

When deck sections serve as stairs, transitions are gradual. A broad step between each of three levels helps define access route. Landscape architect: John Herbst, Jr.

Stairs cascade from upper deck to patio entry below. Mid-level landing is large enough for a bench and planters; angled lower section is both inviting and decorative. Landscape architect: John Herbst, Jr.

SETTING BOUNDARIES

Railings designed for both safety and esthetics

Curvilinear railing *wraps around deck's perimeter. Curved sections are glued up from thin layers of Clear All Heart redwood; edges are rounded over with a router. Design: Eli Sutton & craftsmen Hoddick, Berry & Malakoff.*

Pipe rails *and imposing stuccoed columns, part of home's architecture, securely encircle deck and flank stairways. Architect: Curtis Gelotte Architects.*

This no-rail "railing" is made from tempered glass installed between wooden posts. It keeps kids away from edge and blocks out wind, while preserving view. Landscape architect: Richard E. Harrington.

Curve in railing is created with flexible 1 by 4s and 1 by 6s. Posts, capped with blocks and finials, are built from three sandwiched 2 by 6s (one extends to foundation). Landscape architect: Wallace K. Huntington.

Slant-backed bench doubles as a sturdy side railing. Railing posts are pairs of shaped 2 by 12s bolted to deck's substructure; bench supports are bolted between posts. Design: John McInnis.

Freeform railing traces deck's unusual contours. Ready-made spindles give railing a classic appearance. Design: Gary Marsh.

SITTING PRETTY

Benches that play a variety of roles

Combination bench/railing *runs full length of Japanese-style engawa deck. Treated poles support both bench and deck. Design: Howard A. Kinney.*

Broad, zigzag bench *is made from Clear All Heart redwood 2 by 2s, spaced slightly apart and nailed to a 2 by 4 framework. Front supports are made from 2-inch copper pipe. Design: Eli Sutton.*

Carved into hillside, *bench doubles as retaining wall. Clear All Heart redwood was chosen for both its beauty and its natural resistance to decay. Design: Eli Sutton.*

Hinged bench top opens to reveal handy garden storage center. Solid bench surface keeps out rain. Design: Ed Hoiland.

B

Spaced 1 by 2s make a comfortable, ventilated bench that won't collect water. Design: Herr/Smith Associates.

Sturdy bench, made from standard-size cedar, is heavy but portable enough to move if needed elsewhere. Landscape architect: John Herbst, Jr.

Built-in redwood bench features comfortable backrest, uncluttered design. Posts extend from deck's primary support. Design: Timothy Jones.

DETAILS **39**

DECK SHELTERS

Overheads and screens for shade, privacy, and protection from the elements

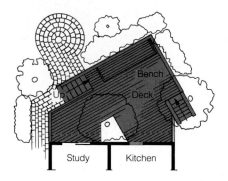

Lath canopy and privacy screen lend a secluded atmosphere to small redwood deck, shielding it from neighboring home's second-story windows. As shown above, deck offers two routes into garden. Landscape architect: Donald G. Boos.

Lattice screen's large picture window lets owners enjoy lofty view of world outside from rooftop garden room. Design: Roy Rydell.

Adjustable louvers of redwood trellis allow homeowners to control shade on southwest side of house. Framework is made of 2 by 8s; 1 by 6 slats pivot on ¼-inch dowels. Design: Brian & Della Zita.

Tall screen of clear acrylic panels blocks wind, but not views. Supports made of 4 by 4s are bolted to deck's substructure. Landscape architect: Ransohoff, Blanchfield & Jones, Inc.

Solid screen, covered with same lap siding as house, offers poolside privacy. Simple spaced-wood trellis caps screen, concealing electrical conduit and extending visual barrier. Landscape architect: John Herbst, Jr.

Angled trellis of widely spaced lath diffuses harsh sun. To support both trellis and swing, 6 by 6 posts extend through redwood decking. Design: Jerome Loston.

PLANTERS

Bringing seasonal color to your deck

Bench-height planter *borders end of deck, offering both greenery and privacy. Angled lines tie planter to bench. Design: Judith L. Donaghey.*

Secure in its macramé cradle, *planter hangs from angled post top. Dowel dropped into notches makes it easy to remove plant for pruning or replanting. Design: Swanson's Nursery & Landscaping.*

Tile-clad redwood planters *and matching benches flank comfortable spa-entertainment deck. Design: John Hemingway.*

Large built-in planters *enhance deck with seasonal color. Though they appear to be quite short, they're actually about 5 feet deep and are made of pressure-treated wood to prevent decay. Landscape architect: John Herbst, Jr.*

STORAGE SPACES

Hiding places for stashing outdoor clutter

Outdoor redwood work counter *offers concealed storage below for recreation equipment. Combining heartwood and sapwood gives structure its distinct appearance. Landscape architect: Richard Splenda & Associates.*

Bench seat *lifts up to reveal handy bins for pots, hoses, and other outdoor equipment. Tightly butted redwood top sheds water. Design: Sol-Era.*

Storage room *below raised deck offers a full head-height "closet" for outdoor gear and pool equipment. For truly sheltered storage, surface above must be watertight. Landscape architect: John Herbst, Jr.*

Trapdoor *in deck surface opens for spa's water-treatment chemicals and equipment. Recessed finger-pull ring lies flat when lid is closed. Design: Judith L. Donaghey.*

Cypress (Select)

Western Red Cedar (Clear)

Western Red Cedar (Select)

Hem-fir (Select)

Galvanized box nails

Redwood (Clear All Heart)

Deck screws

Redwood (Construction Heart)

Deck clips

BUYING MATERIALS

The materials you choose for your deck will affect it in every way, determining not only its looks, but also its function, durability, and cost. For this reason, it's important to be aware of your options, to acquaint yourself with the characteristics of various materials and the differences between them.

This chapter offers information on wood (the most common material) as well as a variety of other choices, such as concrete, tile, and fiberglass. We also discuss substructure and foundation materials, connectors, and fasteners.

If you're not familiar with lumberyard terminology, read the "Lumberyard Primer" on pages 50–51 for comments on lumber grades, species, sizing, and more.

When you select deck materials, start with the topside. Though decks are built from the ground up, they're planned from the top down: the nature and weight of the deck surface governs the type and design of the substructure and foundation.

As you compare materials, balance the cost of each against its appearance, durability, and suitability for your particular design (see pages 52–75 for information on planning your deck).

Lumber and fasteners are at the top of any deck builder's materials list. Shown at left are several popular surfacing species and grades, plus the basic hardware to hold them down. See inside front cover for a comparative guide to softwoods and a chart on softwood grading.

BASIC MATERIALS

Most of your deck-building dollars will go into the materials used for the surface, substructure, and foundation. Some typical choices are described here. Also see the charts on the inside front cover.

SURFACE MATERIALS

Though wood is by far the most common decking surface, other materials may also be used. Sometimes the type of deck demands a different choice; for example, decks requiring watertight surfaces call for special materials (though wooden "duckboards" can be applied over waterproof surfaces). And in some cases, the deck owners may just want a different look. The possibilities are detailed below.

Wood Decking

Perhaps 90 percent of all decks are surfaced with wood—and for good reason. Wood is affordable, relatively lightweight, and easy to work with standard tools; beyond that, it offers natural warmth and beauty. And because it comes in a variety of species, grades, sizes, and textures, lumber allows you to create many decking styles and patterns. For more about

wood, review the "Lumberyard Primer" on pages 50–51.

Other Surfaces

The installation of most nonwood surfacing materials is best left to professionals; you'll often need the help of both a roofer and a mason. Materials that must shelter a room below either provide their own watertight membrane (fiberglass and elastomerics can do this) or go on top of a watertight roof. Watertight roofs are generally covered with hot-mopped asphalt and felt or with a rubberlike, single-ply modified bitumen product before the decking is applied.

As long as the structure is strong enough to support it, almost any patio-surfacing material can go over a watertight roof membrane. If you plan to use heavy masonry, weight will be a major concern: the additional structure needed for support, combined with roofing costs and engineer's fees, can make using these materials quite costly.

Concrete. A deck may be covered with concrete that's troweled smooth and, if desired, tinted or seeded with exposed aggregate gravel. Concrete is highly durable, relatively low in cost,

fire resistant, and maintenance free. But it's *heavy*—a 3-inch-thick slab of "lightweight" concrete weighs about 30 pounds per square foot. Because of their weight, concrete decks must be professionally engineered; to be watertight, they require an underlying roof membrane.

Tile and pavers. Both tile and brick-style pavers are often expensive, but they're hard to surpass for beautiful, elegant-looking surfaces. You'll find a wide range of colors, patterns, and textures, from Mexican terra-cotta to embossed, glazed finishes. The best choices for outdoor decking have a rough, nonslippery finish, stand up well to rugged outdoor use, and don't create glare or heat buildup.

Tile is usually embedded in a mortar-and-wire base on top of hot-mopped asphalt and felt. Brick-style interlocking pavers can go on top of asphalt-impregnated sheathing board that rests on a hot-mopped surface. Because tile and pavers are comparable in weight to concrete, the supporting structure should be professionally designed.

Fiberglass. "Glassing" is another way to obtain a watertight deck surface. Fiberglass costs about the same as all-wood decking; to install it, you put down a special mat (called "roving") over plywood subflooring, then apply coats of polyester resin. The clear resin is often pigmented (to give it some color) and dusted with 30-mesh aggregate sand for traction. Installing fiberglass is generally considered a do-it-yourself project, but if you don't follow the manufacturer's instructions *carefully,* you may end up with a lumpy mess.

On the positive side, a fiberglass deck is durable, termite proof, and rot free (though the subflooring is not); on the down side, it may strongly reflect heat and light (depending upon its color and location), and it must be recoated with resin periodically—every 4 to 5 years.

Handsome redwood deck, *given a clear finish, highlights wood's natural beauty. Wood is the most popular deck-building material because it's affordable, easy to tool, and durable. Design: Bob Flury.*

Elastomeric surface coatings and outdoor carpets. Various kinds of surface coatings, either painted or troweled on, are used as both roofs and finished walking surfaces. These rubberlike substances come in various colors; a nonskid texturing agent is usually mixed into one of the coats. Though it's possible for homeowners to install these membranes themselves, opt for professional application if you want the job to be guaranteed.

Synthetic outdoor carpeting is highly durable and resistant to fading, soil, stain, mildew, fire, and insects. As a deck covering, it offers good traction, deadens sound, and remains cool underfoot on hot days. It isn't watertight, though, and may actually trap water where it can damage surrounding wood. Carpeting also requires more upkeep than other kinds of surface materials.

SUBSTRUCTURE MATERIALS

Beneath a deck's surface, you're likely to find a framework of wooden joists, beams, and posts standing on concrete piers. Special conditions—a need for exceptional strength or durability, for example—call for other materials, such as timber, steel, treated poles, or concrete columns.

Timber

Wood is the most common substructure material. For most elements, you'll use dimension lumber, but especially large beams call for timber—milled lumber with both a width and a thickness of 5 inches or more. Timber is the usual choice for a beam spanning a long distance or a post subject to severe loads.

In place of single-piece timbers, it's possible to use laminated wood structural beams, custom manufactured in straight, arched, or curved shapes; some can span 30 feet or more. Such beams are expensive and generally limited to professionally designed decks.

For a discussion of lumber species, grades, sizes, and other pertinent information, turn to the "Lumberyard Primer" on pages 50–51.

Poles & Piling

Natural poles are particularly attractive, functional posts for decks belonging to rustic cabins and beach houses. Such poles are usually treated with preservatives, but if local codes allow, they may be left untreated or used with the bark attached. Building codes also specify the weights various pole diameters can support.

Decks over sand, mud, or water may be supported by piling—a system of large-diameter steel or specially treated wooden poles. Piling should be designed and installed by professionals, but once it's in place, a do-it-yourselfer can usually complete the rest of the deck.

Steel Structurals

Impervious to fire, rot, and termites, steel posts and beams offer exceptional strength in small dimensions. Because they can cover greater post spans than lumber, they're great for strong, uncluttered substructures.

Due to its high cost, structural steel is often used only for carrying extreme loads or crossing unusually long spans. In addition, most steel structures must be professionally engineered; installation requires welding and (often) the use of special lifts or even a crane. Steel must be painted periodically to prevent rust.

Concrete Columns & Foundations

Some decks are supported by wood posts treated for in-ground use, but most decks stand on concrete footings and piers. In some cases—when a

Perched above the surf, cantilevered deck utilizes heavy timbers for support. Special substructures like this nearly always require engineering. Design: Howard Kinney.

deck is perched on a steep hillside, for example—concrete columns take the place of footings, piers, *and* posts. Strong, fireproof, and impervious to termites and decay, these columns are usually, but not always, cylindrical. Special fiber tubes, available at some masonry yards and home improvement centers, are often used for forming them.

Though working with concrete does involve hard physical labor, fairly small jobs are usually manageable. As a rule, do-it-yourselfers shouldn't attempt to pour concrete columns taller than 3 feet above grade.

FASTENERS & CONNECTORS

Nails, screws, bolts, and metal framing connectors are obviously essential to building—without them, a deck would be nothing but a stack of lumber. Here's a look at the kinds of hardware you'll probably need.

Nails

Nails are sold in boxes (weighing 1, 5, or 50 pounds) or loose in bins. A nail's length is indicated by a "penny" designation ("penny" is abbreviated as "d," from the Latin *denarius*). The equivalents in inches for the most common sizes are as follows:

$$4d = 1\frac{1}{2}"\qquad 6d = 2"\qquad 8d = 2\frac{1}{2}"$$

$$10d = 3"\qquad 16d = 3\frac{1}{2}"\qquad 20d = 4"$$

For exterior use, buy hot-dipped galvanized, aluminum, or stainless steel nails; other types will rust. In fact, even the best hot-dipped nail will rust in time, particularly at the exposed head, where the coating has been battered by your hammer. Stainless steel and aluminum nails won't rust, but they're hard to find (you'll probably have to special-order them) and cost about three times as much as galvanized nails. Aluminum nails are softer than the other types.

You'll find common, box, and finishing nails. Common and box nails, favored for nearly all aspects of deck construction, have extra-thick shanks and broad heads. For more cosmetic connections, where you don't want a nail's head to show (and where strength isn't necessary), choose finishing nails; after driving them nearly flush, you sink the slightly rounded heads with a nailset. Don't secure decking with finishing nails; as the wood naturally swells and shrinks, it will ease the nails upward. And don't use ring-shanked nails; they're practically impossible to remove if bent, or if you need to take up a board later on.

Before you invest in a 50-pound box of nails to put your deck together, you might want to consider renting or buying an air-powered (pneumatic) nailer—it can shrink an all-day nail-

Typical Deck Fasteners

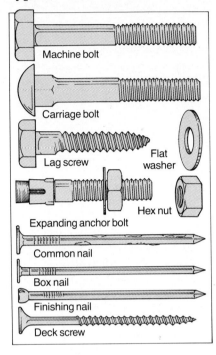

Machine bolt

Carriage bolt

Lag screw

Flat washer

Expanding anchor bolt

Hex nut

Common nail

Box nail

Finishing nail

Deck screw

Bolt & Lag Screw Locations

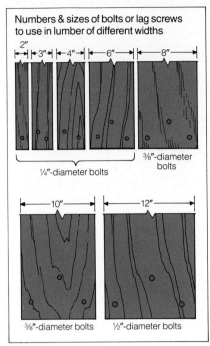

Numbers & sizes of bolts or lag screws to use in lumber of different widths

2" 3" 4" 6" 8"

¼"-diameter bolts

⅜"-diameter bolts

10" 12"

⅜"-diameter bolts ½"-diameter bolts

---

ing job into a single hour and save your arm the corresponding wear and tear. Pneumatic nailers work well for fastening framing together; for redwood or other soft wood decking, stick to hammering by hand, since most pneumatic nailers will set nails too far into the wood. If you do use an air-powered nailer, you'll need to buy special nails joined together in clips, strips, or rings.

Deck Screws

To fasten decking very securely, you can use galvanized deck screws. These long screws have coarse threads and Phillips-slotted heads meant to be driven with a power screwdriver or electric drill with screwdriver tip. For more information on deck screws, see page 88.

Bolts & Lag Screws

For any rigid connection where strength is particularly important

(beam-to-post, ledger-to-house, and so forth), the fasteners of choice are bolts or lag screws.

For decks, you'll be using 3- to 12-inch-long fasteners with diameters from ¼ to ¾ inch (diameter increases in 1/16-inch increments). To accommodate the necessary washers and nuts, bolts should be about 1 inch longer than the combined thickness of the pieces to be bolted together. Plan to predrill bolt holes, using a drill of the same bolt diameter. Use washers under all nuts and under the heads of machine bolts; you don't use them under carriage bolt heads, since the heads of these bolts bite into the wood, keeping the bolt from turning as you tighten the nut.

Lag screws are substitutes for bolts and come in equivalent sizes. They are particularly useful for tight spots where you can reach only one side of the connection with a wrench (a socket wrench is usually most efficient). Plan to drill pilot holes about two-thirds the length of the lag screws, using a drill ⅛ inch smaller in diameter than the lag screw shank. Place a washer under each lag screw's head.

The number and sizes of the bolts and screws depend upon the width of the lumber being joined; typical combinations are shown in the illustration on the facing page. Remember: It's better to form a connection with several small-diameter bolts or lag screws than with fewer fasteners of greater diameter.

For securing ledgers to a masonry wall or anchoring posts to a slab floor, use expanding anchor bolts. These feature expanding shafts or prongs that grip the surrounding hole firmly when the nut is driven home.

Framing Connectors

To the carpenter, few things are more frustrating than watching an angled nail split the end of an expensive piece of lumber. Metal connectors can help you avoid such problems: they make it easier to join materials and also strengthen joints.

Almost any lumberyard offers most of the following framing connectors (and probably several others) in sizes to fit most standard-dimension rough and surfaced lumber. A welder can fabricate similar decorative or specialty supports.

When using framing connectors, be sure to use the sizes and types of nails specified by the manufacturer; in many cases, 16d nails are acceptable.

Joist hangers. Probably the most familiar metal connectors, these make secure butt joints between joists (or rafters) and the load-bearing beam or ledger. Some joist hangers have metal prongs that can be hammered into the side of the joist itself. (The connec-

tion to a beam must be made with nails.)

Post anchors (post bases) secure a load-bearing post to a concrete foundation or slab. In areas where there's much rain or standing water, builders typically choose an elevated post anchor that allows a slight clearance between concrete and wood.

Post caps (post-and-beam connectors) go on top of a post to join it to a beam. They can also strengthen a beam-to-beam splice connection located over a post.

Framing anchors include a kaleidoscope of connectors, each with its own purpose. *Deck clips* allow you to fasten down decking without nailing through the surface. *Reinforcing angles* create solid joints between any two crossing members. *Strapping* (T-straps and L-straps) strengthens a variety of joints.

Framing Connectors

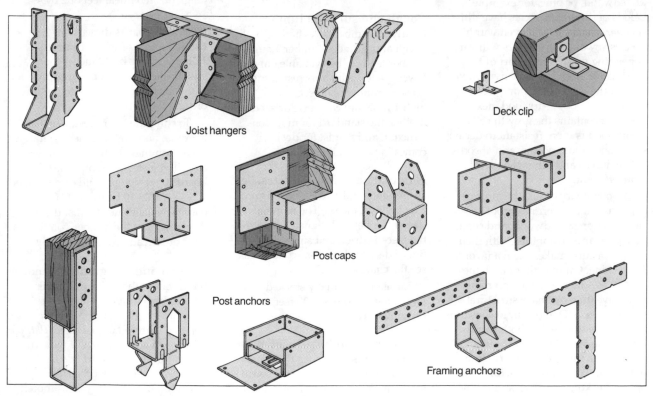

Joist hangers

Deck clip

Post caps

Post anchors

Framing anchors

LUMBERYARD PRIMER

Because the lumber you use strongly influences your deck's appearance and takes the largest bite out of your project dollar, it pays to learn the basics of lumber types and terminology before you visit your lumberyard.

Lumber Terms

Knowing the following terms will help you communicate clearly with the lumberyard attendants.

Softwood and hardwood. All woods belong to one of these two categories. The terms don't refer to a wood's relative hardness, but rather to the kind of tree from which it comes: softwoods come from evergreens (conifers), hardwoods from broadleaf (deciduous) trees. Because hardwoods are generally costlier and more difficult to work with, they're rarely used for deck construction.

Species, heartwood, and sapwood. The particular tree a wood comes from is its species—Douglas fir, redwood, or pine, for example. Woods of different species have different characteristics; and even within a species, a wood's properties will vary depending upon which part of the tree it came from. The inactive wood nearest the center of a living tree is called heartwood. Sapwood, next to the bark, contains the growth cells. Heartwood is more resistant to decay; sapwood is more porous and absorbs preservatives and other chemicals more efficiently.

Among heartwoods, the most decay-resistant and termite-proof species are cypress, redwood, and cedar. This resistance, combined with their natural beauty, makes them a favorite for decking. On the other hand, they tend to be softer, weaker, and more expensive than ordinary structural woods such as Douglas fir or Western larch. To get the best of both worlds, most professional designers favor Douglas fir and the other structural woods for a deck's substructure, but opt for decking, benches, and railings of redwood or cedar. For any wood nearer than 6 inches to the ground or concrete foundations, though, choose one of the decay-resistant heartwoods or pressure-treated woods.

Unseasoned, dry, and kiln-dried lumber. The moisture content of lumber dramatically affects its shrinkage, ability to hold nails, and other important properties. If wood is very damp, it's likely to split, warp, or cup as it dries. Whether air-dried in stacks or kiln-dried, lumber is marked according to its moisture content. S-GRN designates "green" (unseasoned) lumber with a moisture content of 20 percent or more; S-DRY means the moisture content is 19 percent or less; MC 15 lumber is dried to a moisture content of 15 percent or less. Kiln-dried (KD) lumber, though generally drier and less likely to warp, may not be worth the premium you pay for it. No matter how a wood has been dried, it will gain or lose moisture until it adjusts to the moisture content of the surrounding air.

Rough and surfaced lumber. Nearly all lumberyards handle both rough and surfaced lumber. Rough lumber tends to be available only in lower grades, with a correspondingly greater number of defects and a higher moisture content. Surfaced lumber, the standard for most construction and a must for decking, comes in nearly all grades.

Nominal and surfaced sizes. Be aware that a finished "2 by 4" is not 2 inches by 4 inches. The nominal size of lumber is designated before the piece is dried and surfaced; the finished size is less. For actual sizes, see the chart above right.

Lumber is normally stocked in even lengths from 8 to 20 feet, in a broad range of sizes.

Lineal foot and board foot. When lumberyards sell lumber, they do so by either the lineal foot or the board foot. The *lineal foot,* commonly used

STANDARD SOFTWOOD DIMENSIONS

Nominal size	Surfaced (actual) size
1 by 1	¾" by ¾"
1 by 2	¾" by 1½"
1 by 3	¾" by 2½"
1 by 4	¾" by 3½"
1 by 6	¾" by 5½"
1 by 8	¾" by 7¼"
1 by 10	¾" by 9¼"
1 by 12	¾" by 11¼"
2 by 2	1½" by 1½"
2 by 3	1½" by 2½"
2 by 4	1½" by 3½"
2 by 6	1½" by 5½"
2 by 8	1½" by 7¼"
2 by 10	1½" by 9¼"
2 by 12	1½" by 11¼"
4 by 4	3½" by 3½"
4 by 6	3½" by 5½"
4 by 8	3½" by 7¼"
4 by 10	3½" by 9¼"
4 by 12	3½" by 11¼"

for small orders, considers only the *length* of a piece; for example, you might ask for "twenty 2 by 4s, 8 feet long" or "160 lineal feet of 2 by 4."

The *board foot,* on the other hand, takes all a board's dimensions into account: a piece of wood 1 inch thick by 12 inches wide by 12 inches long equals one board foot. The board foot is the most common unit for volume orders.

To compute board feet, use this formula: nominal thickness in inches times nominal width in feet times length in feet. For example, a 2 by 6 board 10 feet long would be computed: 2" x ½' x 10'= 10 board feet. Of course, you still need to list the exact dimensions of the lumber you need so your order can be filled correctly.

Vertical and flat grain. Depending on the cut of the millsaw, lumber will have either parallel grain lines running the length of the boards (*vertical grain*), a marbled appearance (*flat grain*), or a combination of the two. Vertical-grain lumber is less likely to cup and is generally preferred for appearance, but it usually costs more.

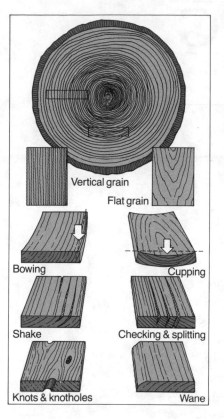

Vertical grain

Flat grain

Bowing

Cupping

Shake

Checking & splitting

Knots & knotholes

Wane

Grades.
Grades. Lumber is sorted and graded at the mill. Generally, lumber grades depend on several factors: natural growth characteristics (such as knots), defects resulting from milling errors, and commercial drying and preserving techniques that affect each piece's strength, durability, and appearance. The illustration above shows typical lumber defects.

A stamp on lumber identifies quality, moisture content, grade name, and (often) species and grading agency (such as WWP for Western Wood Products Association). In most cases, the fewer the knots and other defects, the costlier a board or length of dimension lumber.

Treated Lumber

Though redwood, cedar, and cypress heartwoods resist decay and termites, other woods that contact the earth or trap water will rot and lose their strength. For this reason, less durable types such as Southern pine are often factory-treated with preservatives that guard against rot, insects, and other sources of decay. These woods are generally less expensive, and in many areas more available, than redwood, cedar, and cypress. They can be used for surface decking as well as for strictly structural purposes.

Working with treated lumber isn't always a pleasure. Unlike redwood and cedar, which are easy to cut and nail, treated wood is hard and brittle; it's more difficult to cut and nail, and it warps and twists more readily. Moreover, some people object to its typically greenish cast and the staplelike treatment incisions that usually cover it (some types are available without incising).

And finally, the Environmental Protection Agency has issued precautions about handling chemically treated wood. Because the primary preservative used contains chromium, a toxic metal, you must wear safety goggles and breathing protection when cutting treated lumber, and you should never burn it. For more about preservatives, see page 94.

Plywood

In outdoor construction, plywood is occasionally used for subflooring under waterproof decking. It's also useful for forms for pouring concrete.

Plywood is available in both interior and exterior grades; exterior plywood is best for outdoor use.

Face and back veneers of standard plywood are graded from A through D; A is the highest grade, D the lowest. A/C panels are economical choices where only one side of the plywood will be visible. Face and back grades, glue type, and group number should be stamped on the back or edge of each panel, along with an association trademark that assures quality (such as APA for the American Plywood Association).

Estimating & Ordering Tips

Estimating and ordering materials is not complex, but it's obviously important. Do the job well, and you'll save money; do it carelessly, and you may waste both time and dollars.

Estimating is primarily a matter of measuring and counting the number of pieces necessary. Ballpark estimates made early in your planning will help you compare the costs of different surface and substructure arrangements; a detailed estimate of the final plan provides a basis for ordering materials.

For decking, the following formula will help you calculate how many boards of a specific width will cover the deck's width, assuming a standard ³⁄₁₆-inch spacing between planks:

Number of 2 by 4s laid flat = 3.3 x width of deck in feet

Number of 2 by 6s laid flat = 2.1 x width of deck in feet

Number of 2 by 2s or edge-laid 2 by 3s or 2 by 4s = 7.1 x width of deck in feet

In estimating, round your result to the next highest foot. For example, if you want to cover a 12-foot-wide deck with 2 by 4s, you'll need 3.3 x 12 = 39.6 boards—so you would order at least 40 boards.

No handy rules are available for estimating the amounts needed for a deck's substructure. Just make your estimates from your drawings.

Remember these basic rules for cutting the cost of materials: 1) order as many materials as possible at a single time from a single supplier; 2) choose your supplier on the basis of competitive bids from several retailers; and 3) order materials in regularly available, standard dimensions and in quantities 5 to 10 percent greater than your estimated needs.

If all or part of your construction is being done by a licensed contractor, he or she may arrange to purchase materials for you at a professional discount.

PLANNING YOUR DECK

When you embark upon a project meant to improve your home, it's natural to want to jump right in. Resist the temptation! Planning is your key to success: without it, you're likely to fumble your way through a series of mistakes that are costly and frustrating at best, disastrous at worst.

This chapter takes you through the planning sequence, from evaluating your needs to drawing up construction details. You'll find information on site selection, building codes, plan-drawing techniques, and typical deck construction—from foundations to overheads. For those who don't want to handle the entire design or building process, we also offer some tips on working with professionals (see pages 70–71). Follow the steps outlined here, and you'll formulate the well-thought-out plan you need to tackle your project successfully.

First, consider how your family might use a deck. Do you like to entertain outdoors—and if so, do you need better facilities? Do the children need a flat, dry, comfortable outdoor play area? Would you like to create a poolside place for relaxing? Do you want to enlarge an indoor room by visually extending its floor out into the yard? List all the important factors, then set priorities.

THE RIGHT SITE

Where should you put your deck? An obvious need can quickly determine the best site. For example, if you've been wanting an area off the kitchen where the kids can play and still be supervised from inside, that's probably where you'll build your new deck. Likewise, a cramped dining room may be crying out for an attached deck, or a spa or pool may need a new surround.

Sometimes, though, it isn't so simple to decide where the new deck should go. The following basic considerations will help you pinpoint the right place.

YOUR MICROCLIMATE

If you've lived in your community for a few years, you probably know the general weather conditions: average seasonal temperatures, rainfall and snowfall patterns, prevailing wind directions, and the annual number of sunny days. (If you're a relative new-comer, ask a longtime resident for this information.)

What you may not know, though, are the specifics of your site—how much sunlight will fall on your new deck in July, or where the house casts shadows in spring. Orientation to the weather and the location of obstructions (such as buildings and trees) influence the effects of sun, wind, and rain on different parts of your property, resulting in microclimates that affect the comfort of your deck.

Knowing the sun's path. Theoretically, a deck that faces north is cool because the sun rarely shines on it, while a south-facing deck is usually warm because, from sunrise to sunset, the sun never leaves it. Yards in an eastern exposure stay cool, receiving only morning sunlight; west-facing areas can be uncomfortably hot, since they absorb the full force of the sun's midafternoon rays.

These general rules aren't without exceptions, though. In hot regions of the country, there may be north-facing

decks that could hardly be considered cool in summer. And a west-facing deck in San Francisco is rarely hot, since stiff ocean breezes and chilly fogs are common even during the warmer months.

As shown in the illustration below right, the sun crosses the sky in an arc that changes slightly every day, becoming lower in winter and higher in summer. In the dead of winter, it briefly tracks across the sky at a low angle, throwing long shadows; on long summer days, it moves overhead at a very high angle. As you move farther north from the equator, the difference becomes more dramatic; in Alaska, for example, days are very long in summer, very short in winter.

Using both the drawings and the chart, you can determine where the sun will fall on potential deck locations at various times of year.

Understanding wind. Too much wind can create enough chill on cool days to make a deck unusable. Likewise, if there's no breeze at all, decks in sunny locations can be very uncomfortable in summer weather.

Your deck's location or design may be influenced by three different kinds of winds: annual prevailing winds, very localized seasonal breezes, and occasional high-velocity winds generated by stormy weather. Even if your proposed deck faces strong winds only occasionally, you may have to

Seasonal Sun Angles

	Season	Sun's Position/Hours of Daylight (see map below)		
		Area 1	Area 2	Area 3
A	Noon, 12/21	21°/8 hrs.	29°/9 hrs.	37°/10 hrs.
B	Noon, 3/21 & 9/21	45°/12 hrs.	53°/12 hrs.	60°/12 hrs.
C	Noon, 6/21	69°/16 hrs.	76°/15 hrs.	83°/14 hrs.

Plotting the Sun's Path

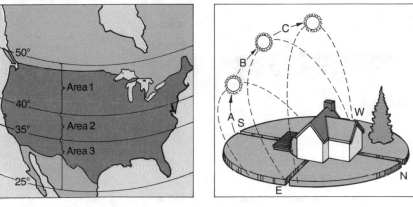

Shade is cast at various angles, depending on time of year and where you live. Find your location on map, then refer to chart for sun angles on your property.

strengthen its foundations and sub-structure. If it receives mild prevailing breezes, you may wish to modify their effects with vertical screens or fences, as illustrated in the four drawings below.

A house is a formidable wind-break. Where regular breezes are a problem, you can shelter your deck by locating it on the side of the house opposite the direction of prevailing winds.

Reckoning with the rain. Though you're unlikely to use your deck during poor weather, it will take a beating—and age more rapidly—if it's pounded by frequent rains. As you evaluate deck locations, note which way the house roof is pitched; that's where runoff might occur. If necessary, runoff can

be redirected with gutters. Preventing water penetration is especially important with rooftop decks. For more information, see page 75.

Dealing with snow. In areas that experience heavy snowfall, even if only sporadically, any deck must be capable of handling the snow's added weight. Snow is surprisingly heavy; piled 5 to 6 feet deep, it can weigh as much as 80 to 100 pounds per square foot—twice the maximum deck load allowed by building codes in many mild-climate regions. This standing weight alone can be enough to collapse an improperly designed structure.

If you live in an area where it snows, be sure to consult a professional about your deck's structural requirements.

PHYSICAL ASSETS

When siting your deck, think carefully about how you'd like it to relate to both house and yard.

Relationship to the house. Unless you want a private deck away from the household hubbub, quick and easy access from the house is important. Evaluate each potential site's accessibility, considering established traffic patterns from house to yard, locations of doors (both present and future), and overall convenience. Remember: If a deck isn't in a convenient place, it may go unused.

Don't forget to take into account what's below a possible high-level location. A high-level deck will cool

Effective Wind Barriers

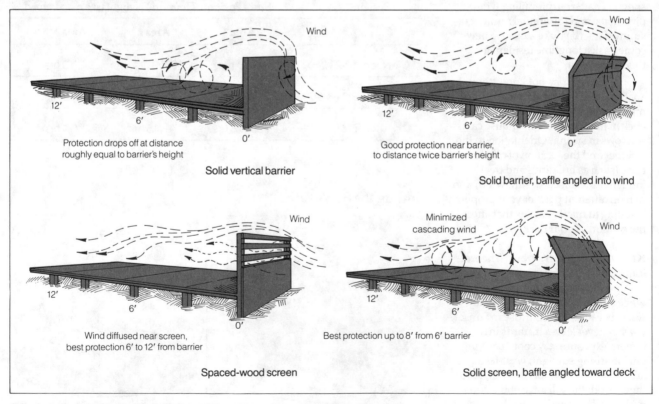

Protection drops off at distance roughly equal to barrier's height

Solid vertical barrier

Good protection near barrier, to distance twice barrier's height

Solid barrier, baffle angled into wind

Wind diffused near screen, best protection 6' to 12' from barrier

Spaced-wood screen

Minimized cascading wind

Best protection up to 8' from 6' barrier

Solid screen, baffle angled toward deck

Wind-control studies indicate that a solid screen or fence isn't necessarily the best barrier against wind; angled baffles or lattice-type fencing are better choices. Fence-top baffle aimed into wind offers the most shelter; lattice-type screen provides diffused protection near fence.

and shade the area it overhangs; it may block light and transmit noise, and its substructure may obstruct views. One the other hand, it can provide a perfect site for covered storage.

Relationship to the yard. Study your yard—the contours, views, locations of trees and any other relevant elements—and try to maximize its assets. At the same time, don't ignore any drawbacks, such as drop-offs, overly shady spots, exposures to blazing sun or strong winds, and areas with poor drainage or unstable soil. Though a deck can often be designed to deal with or even solve such problems, it may be more expensive to build because of them.

LEGAL LIMITS

Before you've gone too far in planning your deck, consult your local building department for any legal restrictions. In most areas, you'll need to file for a building permit and comply with building code requirements. Also be aware of local zoning ordinances, which normally govern whether or not a deck can be built on your land and where it can be located.

Building permits. Before you pound a single nail, get the needed permits. It's important that the building office check plans before construction begins, to ensure that you don't get off to a substandard start. Procrastination or negligence may come back to haunt you: officials can fine you and require you to bring an illegally built structure up to standard or even to dismantle it entirely.

The need for a permit generally hinges on a deck's size and intended use, and on whether or not it's attached to the house. In most areas, any house-attached or freestanding deck more than 30 inches off the ground requires a permit and must be built according to building codes. If the project includes any electrical wiring or plumbing, you may need a separate permit for each of these.

Fees are usually charged for permits. These fees are generally determined by the projected value of the improvement—so when you apply for a permit, be as accurate as possible about the estimated cost. If you overestimate, you might push the fee higher. Many building offices figure a project's value based on standardized construction costs per square foot.

Building codes set minimum safety standards for materials and construction techniques: depth of footings (shown in the illustration below), size of beams, and proper fastening methods, for example. Code requirements ensure that any structures you build will be well made and safe for your family and any future owners of your property.

Zoning ordinances restrict the height of residential buildings, limit lot coverage (the proportion of the lot a building or group of buildings may cover), specify setbacks (how close to the property lines you can build), and—in some areas—stipulate architectural design standards.

Decks rarely exceed height limitations, but they're often affected by setback requirements. They also increase

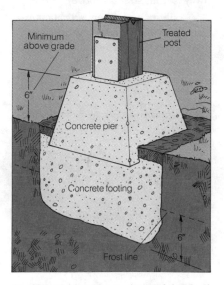

Building codes govern size and depth of deck foundations and set other, similar standards.

Zoning Restrictions

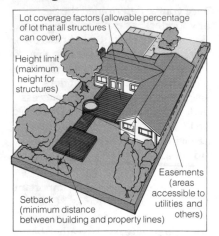

In many areas, zoning ordinances control setbacks, lot coverage, and building heights.

your overall lot coverage—an important consideration, since a deck might negate future additions to your home.

Variances. If the zoning department rejects your plans, you can apply for a variance at your city or county planning department. It's your task to prove to a hearing officer or zoning board of appeal that following the zoning requirements precisely would create "undue hardship," and that the structure you want to build will not negatively affect either your neighbors or the community. If you plead your case convincingly, you'll be allowed a variance.

Architectural review boards. Neighborhoods with tight controls may require that your improvement meet certain architectural standards—and that means submitting your plans to an architectural review board. Be advised that going through this process can dramatically increase the time required to get your project moving.

Deeds. Your property deed can also restrict your project's design, construction, or location. Review the deed carefully, checking for easements, architectural-standard restrictions, and other limitations.

INITIAL DESIGN

Once you've determined the best site for your deck, as explained on pages 53–55, it's time to put your ideas on paper and boil them down into a workable design. Before you begin, gather as much information about deck design as you can: study the successful deck designs pictured in this book, flip through home improvement magazines to see more examples, and see as many decks as you can at the homes of friends and neighbors.

As discussed earlier, it's important to design a deck that "works." Good looks alone are not enough; your deck must also survive harsh weather, blend with the house, coordinate with interior rooms, and stay put during wind storms or earthquakes. To achieve all these goals, you must use appropriate techniques and materials. For help in selecting materials, review the chapter beginning on page 45; remember that you need durable, affordable materials that comply with codes and offer the look that's right for your home. For information on building techniques, turn to page 76.

Whether you intend to do the actual construction yourself or bid the project out to contractors, make all your plans as complete as possible to minimize confusion later.

BASIC DRAWING

It doesn't take an artist to design a simple deck. In fact, the process is more science than art: once you gather a few basic drawing tools and attain a clear understanding of what must be done, you're halfway there. If you don't have a drawing board, T-square, and triangles, a tablet of graph paper and a ruler will do.

Understanding "views." A deck's basic surface pattern and substructure should be drawn separately in plan view (seen from above, looking straight down). Arrangement of the substructure should be drawn in both plan view and elevation view (seen

Typical Drawing Views

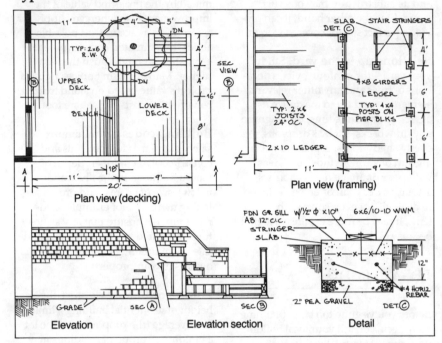

Plan view (decking)

Plan view (framing)

Elevation

Elevation section

Detail

straight-on from one side). To simplify confusing portions of the deck, you may need to draw them in a section view as well; this is like an elevation view with part of the structure cut away (see illustration above).

Railings and other vertical members are best drawn in elevation view. Attachments and other details should

be drawn from the view that most clearly shows their construction; three-dimensional detail sketches sometimes work best for these.

Drawing to scale. To reduce your future deck's plan to paper size accurately, you draw it to scale. For this type of project, a typical scale for plan and

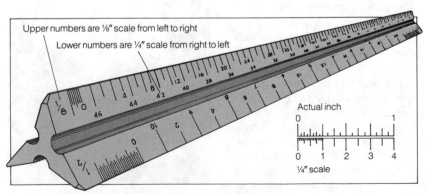

Architectural scale ruler makes it easy to reduce a drawing to a smaller scale. Most have markings for several different scale reductions.

elevation views reduces each foot of the actual deck to ¼ or ½ inch, depending upon the deck's size. To make the drawing job easier, you can use an architectural scale ruler, which has dimension markings for a variety of scales (see drawing at bottom of facing page).

Another way to draw to scale is to use graph paper; a scale in which 6 squares equal 1 foot (6:1) works well for deck surfacing patterns and general arrangements of joists, beams, and posts. For benches, railings, and other details, the easiest scale to work with is 12:1—that is, 12 squares equal 1 foot (and one square equals 1 inch). If you need a larger drawing area than one sheet provides, tape several sheets of graph paper together.

BASE MAP

Even if you intend to hire a professional to design your deck (see pages 70–71), it's still wise to draw up a base map—a plan of your existing property and house. This can save you money by streamlining your designer's work; it also gives you a background for sketching out various deck configurations so you can communicate your ideas clearly. Of course, if you can locate architect's drawings or deed maps that show the actual dimensions and orientation of your property, you can eliminate this step (and save yourself considerable work).

Base map data. Using a 50- or 100-foot tape measure, measure the area where your deck will be located, plotting out the following features and their dimensions. Make a rough sketch first; then transfer the information to a more refined scale drawing, being sure to include these elements:

■ Dimensions of your lot

■ Location of the house and other structures, such as pool, spa, or garage

■ Doors, windows, and interior house walls

Base Map

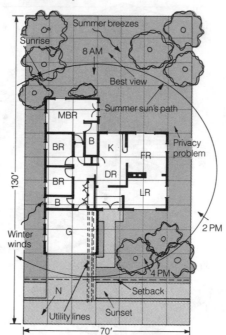

Final base map shows all the factors that may affect deck placement.

■ Points on the compass

■ Path and direction of the sun and any garden "hot spots"

■ Utility lines (water, gas, and sewer) and the depth of each; underground wires

■ Setback lines

■ Direction of prevailing winds

■ Existing trees and large plants

■ Any obstructions beyond the lot that may affect sun, view, or privacy

SKETCHING DECK CONFIGURATIONS

Arm yourself with a good supply of tracing paper and a pencil, then start testing possible deck configurations: place a sheet of paper over your base map, sketch in a deck, and evaluate it. If you're not pleased, just start over again with a fresh piece of paper. Don't confine your ideas to rectangles or single-level decks—even though such decks are more economical to build, they may not be the best, most interesting choices for you. A little extra expense and work in designing and building can pay off in a more satisfying result.

Once you've created a shape that seems to work, figure the deck's actual size and confirm its shape and placement at the site. Then refine your scale drawing. As you move closer to your final design, be sure to consider traffic patterns. Foot traffic should move smoothly from house to deck to garden. If you have to open up a wall to improve circulation, avoid producing traffic patterns that run through the middle of rooms (see drawings below).

Controlling Foot Traffic

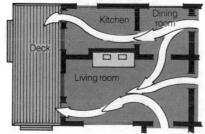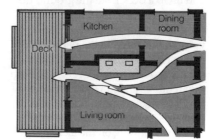

Foot traffic that moves from house to deck through centers of rooms is awkward and disruptive, as shown at left. Best traffic pattern flows along room perimeters (see at right).

SURFACE & SUBSTRUCTURE

When you've sketched your ideas, you're ready to design the deck's surface and supporting framework. (If you're not handy at design work, this is a good time to consult a pro for help; see pages 70–71.) Unless the framework is quite low, it's usually a good idea to draw it in both plan and elevation views. When you draw the elevations, it may be necessary to illustrate from the front and one side.

In their basic structure, most decks resemble one or both of the decks shown in the illustration at the bottom of the facing page. Footings support piers, which hold posts. Beams run from post to post; joists span from beam to beam, either running across the tops of beams or hanging between them for a lower profile. House-attached decks connect to a ledger mounted on a wall. Decking lumber spans across the tops of the joists.

There are exceptions to the rule, of course, including decks built directly on patio slabs (see page 74) and roof decks (see page 75). And even decks similar to those shown in the drawing won't be exactly identical to them. Because there is so much variation, it's important to understand construction techniques clearly at this stage. Now is the time to read through the following design options and page through the techniques section beginning on page 76.

SURFACE DESIGN

You build a deck from the ground up, but it's usually best to design it from the decking surface down. That way, you can first develop the part you see and use, then figure out how to support it. To keep from creating a pattern that requires an impractical structure, you'll need to understand support practices, so read through the information beginning on the facing page before starting.

Most decks are surfaced with standard sizes of dimension lumber:

Deck Surface Patterns

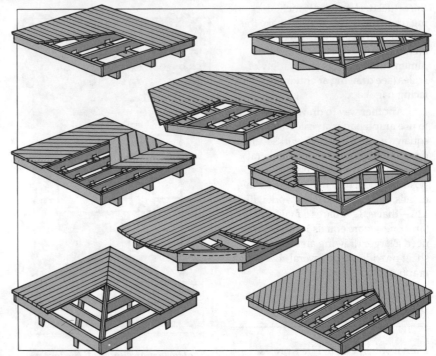

Diagonal, checkerboard, herringbone: decking may be laid in a variety of patterns. Pattern you choose will determine proper configuration of supporting joists and beams.

surfaced 2 by 6s, 2 by 4s, or 2 by 3s. Two by 2s tend to twist and warp easily; 2 by 8s (and anything larger) tend to cup and drain poorly.

The simplest, soundest, and most economical decking patterns are those in which 2 by 6s or 2 by 4s are laid parallel and running the deck's full length or width, but lumber can also be arranged in many other patterns. For example, you might mix lumber of two or more different widths, such as 2 by 4s and 2 by 6s. Or you can create on-edge patterns by laying 2 by 3s or 2 by 4s on their edges, usually directly on beams (without joists), as shown at the top of the facing page. On-edge decking is heavy and expensive, but it can span long distances between supports—an advantage if you want to pare down the substructure. (Be aware, though, that the added expense of this sort of decking pattern generally isn't

offset by the substructure savings.)

As you develop your pattern, keep these points in mind:

■ Support must be provided under both ends of each piece and along its length at intervals determined by the decking lumber's thickness, grade, and species. Generally speaking, the more complex the pattern, the more complicated the substructure must be to support it. Examples of frameworks for various decking patterns are illustrated above. It's best to stagger end joints when lengths of lumber must be joined end to end.

■ You can minimize waste by designing for standard lumber lengths from 8 to 20 feet, in 2-foot increments.

■ Decking lumber should be spaced from ³⁄₁₆ to ³⁄₈ inch apart to allow for drainage, ventilation, and the natural

Parallel Deck Patterns

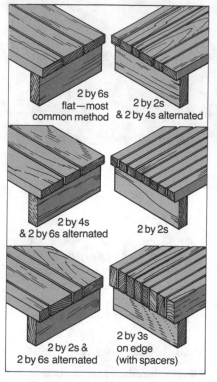

2 by 6s
flat—most
common method

2 by 2s
& 2 by 4s alternated

2 by 4s
& 2 by 6s alternated

2 by 2s

2 by 2s &
2 by 6s alternated

2 by 3s
on edge
(with spacers)

Decking boards may be laid flat or, for longer spans, on edge; widths may be alternated.

expansion and contraction of the wood.

■ A "2 by 6" is not 2 inches by 6 inches. Nominal dimensions of surfaced lumber designate the size before drying and surfacing; actual dimensions are about ½ inch smaller in thickness and width. Thus, a 2 by 6 is really only 1½ by 5½ inches, a 4 by 4 is really only 3½ by 3½ inches, and so on. See the chart on page 50 for the list of actual sizes of surfaced lumber.

To evaluate possible decking patterns, sketch them on tracing paper laid on top of your scale drawing of the deck's shape; be aware that an intricate pattern can be expensive to build and may overwhelm a small deck. When you've settled on a pattern that you like and that works well for your deck, draw it in plan view.

SUBSTRUCTURE DESIGN

Based on the construction technique you choose, develop a framing and foundation system. Here are the elements you'll need to consider.

Joists

Deck joists—typically 2 by 6s, 2 by 8s, 2 by 10s, or 2 by 12s on edge—spread decking loads across beams, making it possible to use decking materials that otherwise couldn't span the distances between beams. (Some designs eliminate joists, utilizing only beams and on-edge 2 by 3 or 2 by 4 decking.) Joists can either sit on top of beams and ledgers or connect to the faces of these supports.

You'll want to cap the ends of joists resting on top of a beam with rim joists (see illustration below). When figuring joist lengths, be sure to allow for the added thickness of the cap.

Joists that support standard-spaced wooden decking are mounted level, but those supporting solid, watertight materials must slope to allow for rain runoff. For more on this subject, see page 89.

Beams (or Girders)

Beams may be solid lumber or built up from lengths of 2-by dimension lumber fastened together. Large beams are usually easiest to handle if they're built up, since they can be carried to their final destination in pieces. However, a single, solid beam is generally favored for a highly visible location.

The beam spans given in the table on page 63 are for sawed lumber, such as a 4 by 6 that measures 3½ by 5½ inches after surfacing. You cannot build an equally strong beam by sand-

Typical Deck Construction

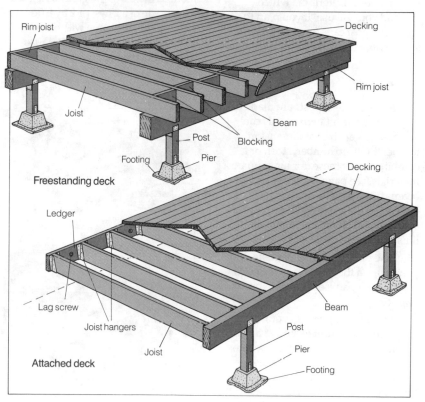

Rim joist

Decking

Rim joist

Joist

Beam

Post

Blocking

Footing

Pier

Freestanding deck

Ledger

Decking

Lag screw

Beam

Joist hangers

Post

Pier

Joist

Footing

Attached deck

Post & Beam Connections

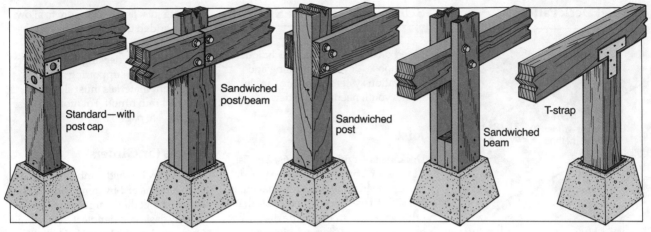

Standard—with post cap

Sandwiched post/beam

Sandwiched post

Sandwiched beam

T-strap

wiching two 2 by 6s, because together they measure only 3 inches (twice the thickness of 1½ inches) by 5½ inches. Another point to keep in mind is that in many areas, wood beams positioned within 6 inches of the ground must be made from pressure-treated or decay-resistant lumber.

Beams can be fastened to posts using any of several methods, as shown above. Determine which method you will use. If you plan to use metal post caps (see page 49), be sure to note them in your design.

Posts

Though most deck posts are made of 4 by 4s, various other materials can be used: larger sizes of dimension lumber, built-up lumber, steel, or a combination of these (for more on post materials, see page 47). Posts and beams often mesh—for example, built-up posts are designed to capture beams by sandwiching them (see illustration above).

The proper spacing of posts depends upon the distances the deck's beams can span; see the table on page 63.

During this phase of your design work, you may want to study various configurations for overheads, screens, railings, and benches (see pages 64–69). To provide the sturdiest support for these, extend the main posts

through the deck surface and up to the necessary height.

Ledgers

A ledger is a plank or beam mounted to a house wall, adjoining deck, or similar structure; it receives and supports one end of a deck's joists, as shown below. When a ledger is placed within about 36 inches of the ground, it is often made of a 2 by 6 or 2 by 8 (ledgers are generally the same width or one size larger than the joists). Because taller decks require sturdier support,

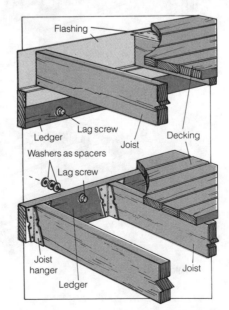

Flashing

Lag screw

Ledger

Washers as spacers

Lag screw

Joist

Decking

Joist hanger

Ledger

Joist

their ledgers are usually best made from a 4-by—a 4 by 8 or 4 by 10, for example. If a ledger is in contact with earth, concrete, or masonry, it should be made from decay-resistant or pressure-treated lumber.

Bridging & Bracing

Despite the inherent strength in a deck's basic members, bridging and bracing are important for a stable structure. *Bridging or blocking* between joists keeps them from twisting or moving; *bracing* provides lateral stability for tall posts.

Bridging or blocking joists. Long spans and wide spacing may allow joists to twist or buckle unless they're cross braced with bridging or blocking. The joist width is also a consideration; 2 by 12 to 2 by 8 joists require more blocking than 2 by 6s.

The need for blocking is determined by local codes. Typically, it's a good idea to block between joists over any beams or load-bearing members. In addition, joists spanning more than 8 feet require blocking every 8 feet; those with spans over 12 feet need at least two rows of blocking. For joist spans less than 8 feet, rim joists nailed across the joist ends are adequate.

Bracing posts. Though building codes govern the need to brace posts,

Bridging & Blocking

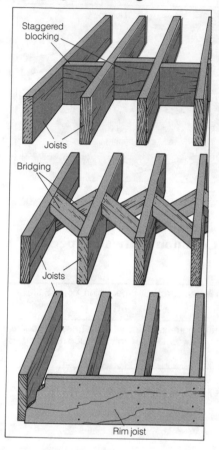

Staggered blocking

Joists

Bridging

Joists

Rim joist

Foundation

Almost all decks are supported by a basic foundation that anchors the substructure against settling, slippage, and wind lift; distributes loads into the ground; and protects posts from direct contact with the earth. A typical foundation has two parts: concrete piers and footings (or their equivalents). Building codes govern the size and spacing of foundations and specify how deep into the ground they go.

A footing should be about twice the width of the pier it supports. Typical footings are 12 inches square and 6 to 8 inches thick; 6 inches of the thickness extends below the frost line.

Concrete piers, often formed and poured at the same time the footings are poured, may be cylindrical, rectangular, or pyramidal with flat tops. The top surface must be large enough to hold metal post anchors or nailing blocks with room to spare. Once in place, piers should be exposed about 6 inches above ground. See page 79 for information on foundations.

Bracing Posts

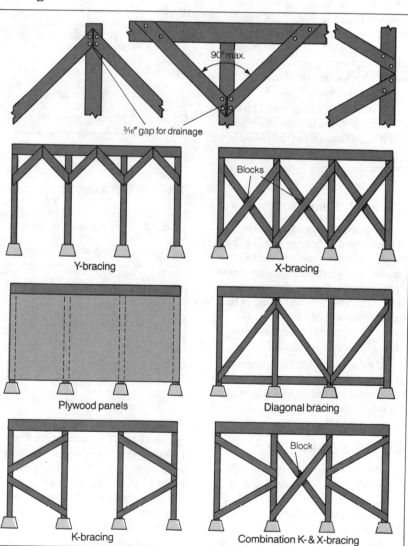

90° max.

³⁄₁₆" gap for drainage

Y-bracing

X-bracing

Blocks

Plywood panels

Diagonal bracing

K-bracing

Combination K- & X-bracing

Block

you can count on bracing any posts that support any of the following:

■ Freestanding decks over 36 inches above ground

■ Attached decks taller than 12 feet

■ Any deck (regardless of height) projecting farther than 20 feet from the house (or projecting for more than twice the length of the attached side)

■ Decks exposed to high winds, seismic activity, or heavy loads

If the deck height is less than 12 feet, only outside posts on the unattached sides of the substructure will normally need cross bracing; plan to use 2 by 4s across distances less than 8 feet, 2 by 6s for greater distances. Fasten the cross braces to the posts with bolts or lag screws. Various bracing methods are illustrated at right.

Deck Loads

A deck's framework must be designed in accordance with guidelines for allowable loading. Otherwise, under pressure from unusual stresses—heavy snow or a large party, for example—the structure may not stay in one piece.

Though building codes vary, many areas require that a substructure be strong enough to support 40 pounds of live load plus 10 pounds of dead weight (the weight of the construction materials) per square foot. The tables and other design information given here are based on this "40 plus 10 p.s.f." loading at deck heights up to 12 feet. Keep in mind that this information is developed from the Uniform Building Code (UBC) and other sources that may not meet all local code requirements. Use these tables for planning and design, but be sure to check with your building department as well.

If your deck will be over 12 feet above grade (even at only one post), or if it must bear abnormally weighty loads, have your plans checked by a structural engineer.

Allowable Spans & Spacings

A span is the distance bridged by planks, joists, or beams; spacing is the distance between adjacent joists, beams, or posts (see illustration above right). Because they determine the ultimate strength or weakness of the support system, carefully figured spans and spacings are critical to proper substructure design.

As the tables illustrate, the maximum safe spans and spacings for lumber of different dimensions depend on the wood species and grade you use.

Using the Tables

Use the five tables here to figure the proper sizes, spans, spacings, and heights for your deck's structural elements. As you work through the tables from 1 through 5, you'll see that any of several joist-beam-post combinations

Spans & Spacings

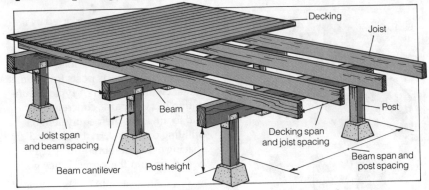

Table 1: Strength Groupings of Common Softwood Species

(Based on No. 2 & Better)

Group A	Douglas fir, Western hemlock, Western larch, Southern pine, coast Sitka spruce
Group B	Western cedar, Douglas fir (South), hem-fir, Alpine white fir, Eastern mountain hemlock, pine (all but Southern), redwood (Clear only), spruce (Eastern, Engelmann, Sitka)
Group C	Northern white cedar, redwood (Construction Heart & Better)

Table 2: Decking Spans

Dimensions shown are maximum suggested decking spans (or joist spacings). Greater spans are possible with some sizes, but may result in a deck that seems overly springy underfoot. Spans assume normal loads, distributed evenly across several boards.

	Species Group (see Table 1)		
	A	B	C
Nominal 1-inch boards laid flat	16"	14"	12"
Nominal 2-inch lumber laid flat	24"	24"	24"
2 by 3s laid on edge	48"	36"	32"
2 by 4s laid on edge	60"	60"	60"

will work for a given situation. For example, 4 by 8 beams spaced 10 feet apart may call for supporting posts every 6 feet; if spaced just 4 feet apart, the same beams would require posts only every 10 feet along their lengths. Some combinations are more economical and attractive than others, since

they require less lumber, smaller or easier-to-handle beam sizes, less space, or fewer footings. Also keep in mind that the figures given in the tables are maximum limits; you can always choose shorter spans, closer spacings, or larger joists, beams, and posts.

Table 3: Maximum Joist Spans & Spacings

Spans are from center to center of beams or supports based on No. 2 & Better joists placed on edge.

	Maximum Span per Species Group (see Table 1)		
	A	B	C
16" joist spacings:			
2 by 6	9'9"	8'7"	7'9"
2 by 8	12'10"	11'4"	10'2"
2 by 10	16'5"	14'6"	13'
24" joist spacings:			
2 by 6	8'6"	7'6"	6'9"
2 by 8	11'3"	9'11"	8'11"
2 by 10	14'4"	12'8"	11'4"
32" joist spacings:			
2 by 6	7'9"	6'10"	6'2"
2 by 8	10'2"	9'	8'1"
2 by 10	13'	11'6"	10'4"

Table 5: Wood Post Sizes & Heights

Proper post size depends on overall load area and post height. To figure load area, multiply beam spacing by post spacing. Round up to next largest load area listed below. Sizes are based on Standard & Better for 4 by 4 posts, No. 1 & Better for larger sizes.

Species Group (see Table 1)	Post Size (nominal)	Load Area									
		36	48	60	72	84	96	108	120	132	144
A	4 by 4	Up to 12' high →					Up to 10' high →		Up to 8' high →		
	4 by 6						Up to 12' →			Up to 10' →	
	6 by 6										Up to 12'
B	4 by 4	Up to 12' →		Up to 10' →		Up to 8' →					
	4 by 6			Up to 12' →			Up to 10' →				
	6 by 6							Up to 12' →			
C	4 by 4	Up to 12'	Up to 10' →		Up to 8' →			Up to 6' →			
	4 by 6			Up to 12' →		Up to 10' →		Up to 8' →			
	6 by 6					Up to 12' →					

Table 4: Beam Sizes & Spans

Because a series of beams generally must share the overall load of a deck, proper beam spans depend on beam spacing.

Spans—center-to-center distances between posts or supports—are based on No. 2 & Better beams placed on edge.

Species Group (see Table 1)	Beam Size (nominal)	Spacing between Beams (Joist Span)								
		4'	5'	6'	7'	8'	9'	10'	11'	12'
A	4 by 6	Up to 6' spans →								
	3 by 8	Up to 8' →		Up to 7'	Up to 6' →					
	4 by 8	Up to 10'	Up to 9'	Up to 8'	Up to 7' →		Up to 6' →			
	3 by 10	Up to 11'	Up to 10'	Up to 9'	Up to 8' →		Up to 7' →		Up to 6' →	
	4 by 10	Up to 12'	Up to 11'	Up to 10'	Up to 9' →		Up to 8' →		Up to 7' →	
	3 by 12		Up to 12'	Up to 11'	Up to 10'	Up to 9' →		Up to 8' →		
	4 by 12			Up to 12' →		Up to 11'	Up to 10' →		Up to 9' →	
	6 by 10					Up to 12'	Up to 11'	Up to 10' →		
B	4 by 6	Up to 6' →								
	3 by 8	Up to 7' →		Up to 6' →						
	4 by 8	Up to 9'	Up to 8'	Up to 7' →		Up to 6' →				
	3 by 10	Up to 10'	Up to 9'	Up to 8'	Up to 7' →		Up to 6' →			
	4 by 10	Up to 11'	Up to 10'	Up to 9'	Up to 8' →		Up to 7' →			Up to 6'
	3 by 12	Up to 12'	Up to 11'	Up to 10'	Up to 9'	Up to 8' →		Up to 7' →		
	4 by 12		Up to 12'	Up to 11'	Up to 10' →		Up to 9' →		Up to 8' →	
	6 by 10			Up to 12'	Up to 11'	Up to 10' →		Up to 9' →		
C	4 by 6	Up to 6'								
	3 by 8	Up to 7'	Up to 6'							
	4 by 8	Up to 8'	Up to 7'	Up to 6' →						
	3 by 10	Up to 9'	Up to 8'	Up to 7'	Up to 6' →					
	4 by 10	Up to 10'	Up to 9'	Up to 8' →		Up to 7' →		Up to 6' →		
	3 by 12	Up to 11'	Up to 10'	Up to 9'	Up to 8'	Up to 7' →			Up to 6' →	
	4 by 12	Up to 12'	Up to 11'	Up to 10'	Up to 9' →		Up to 8' →		Up to 7' →	
	6 by 10		Up to 12'	Up to 11'	Up to 10'	Up to 9' →		Up to 8' →		

AMENITIES

Once you've planned your deck's surface and basic substructure, it's time to consider amenities such as railings, stairs, overheads, benches, and so forth. Here are some design suggestions for these components.

RAILINGS & SCREENS

The strongest railings and screens are those connecting to posts that extend up from the deck's substructure. Unfortunately, though, it isn't always practical to integrate these elements

into the deck design. A few typical designs are shown below and on the facing page; you'll find more ideas on pages 32–43.

Be sure to coordinate railings and screens with your house's architectural style: use similar materials, connections, and detailing. Also consult building codes for technical data on railing heights, stair tread sizes, and so forth to be sure the information given here complies with your regulations.

Railings are generally required for decks over 36 inches high and for any flights of stairs. Multilevel decks can

sometimes go without if each level is at least 36 inches deep from front to back (so that each level becomes a deck unto itself), but even in these cases, railings are strongly recommended.

Railings are generally 36 to 42 inches above a deck's surface; they must be built strongly enough to resist a hefty horizontal force (up to 20 pounds per square foot). Both railings and screens can have rails, pickets, louvers, or any number of solid facings such as plywood siding, shingles, stucco, plastic panels, or tempered glass.

Railing Designs

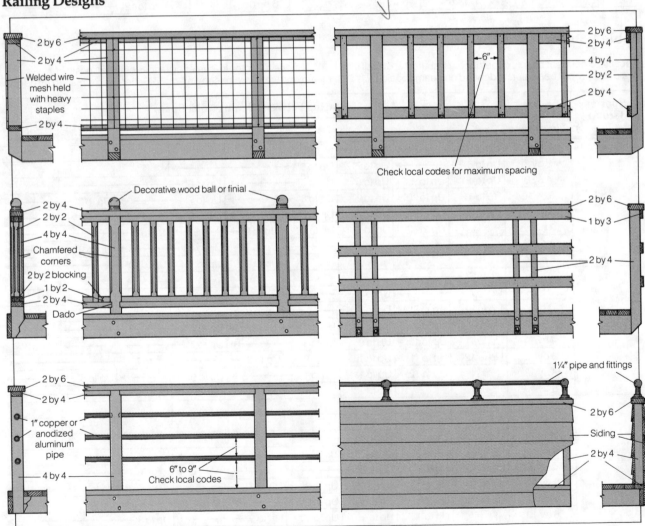

Screen Designs

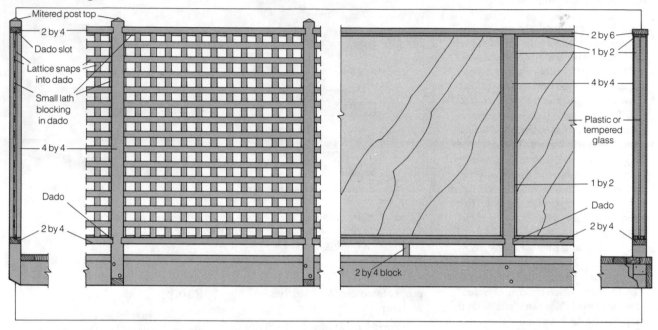

Mitered post top
2 by 4
Dado slot
Lattice snaps into dado
Small lath blocking in dado
4 by 4
Dado
2 by 4

2 by 6
1 by 2
4 by 4
Plastic or tempered glass
1 by 2
Dado
2 by 4

2 by 4 block

Basic structure. Regardless of design, railings and screens have the same basic structure: vertical posts capped and joined by a cross member laid flat. The cross member (the cap) may be the same width or wider than the posts. The spacing between posts depends on the cap's size and the horizontal rail's length, though 4 by 4 posts can generally be spaced up to 4 feet apart under a 2 by 4 cap, up to 6 feet apart under a 2 by 6.

Rail-to-post connections. The strongest and simplest railings and screens are those with horizontal members screwed or bolted to the outside faces of posts; however, you can create a cleaner, more streamlined railing by placing horizontals between the posts.

STAIRS, RAMPS & MULTILEVELS

Stairs, ramps, and changes in level all help your deck blend with the house and landscape. They offer access, guide foot traffic, and help the deck follow ground contours; stairs and level changes can also provide bonus seating and simply add visual interest. For safety, utility, and esthetics, these elements should comply with specific design rules, as outlined below.

Low-level decks less than a foot or two above grade tie nicely into a garden, especially when deck-wide steps, ramps, or linked levels of decking are used to connect the main deck with the yard. Steps running the deck's full length or width also serve to hide views of the support structure.

Stair Design

Here are a few guidelines for designing safe, convenient stairs. Refer to the drawing at right for typical terminology.

Passage width. Decide how much traffic you expect, then base your stairs' passage width on the following minimums for general access: provide at least 4 feet for one person, 5 feet for two abreast; add 2 feet per person for greater numbers of side-by-side users. Service stairs or other deliberately restricted access may have a minimum passage width of 2 feet.

Run. Steps and stairs for elevation changes up to about 8 feet can generally be handled in a single straight, uninterrupted run stretching directly from one level to another. For a higher total rise, a landing makes climbing easier, and a change in direction

Stair Jargon

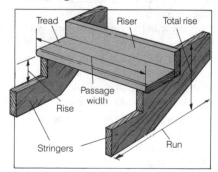

Tread
Riser
Total rise
Passage width
Rise
Stringers
Run

makes the stairs less imposing. L- and U-shaped runs with landings are recommended in these situations.

Treads, risers, and stringers. For steps to be safe and comfortable to use, the tread width and riser height must maintain a particular relationship: as risers become shorter, treads should grow wider (see illustration at right).

For outdoor steps, twice the riser height added to the tread width should equal 26 inches. The ideal riser height for standard stairs is considered to be 7 inches, but the riser/tread relationship you choose will depend upon how heavily you expect the stairs to be used for access. When figuring tread dimensions, measure the tread from riser to riser and disregard any overhang. Three 2 by 4s spaced ¼ inch apart make a tread of 11 inches; two 2 by 6s with ¼-inch spacing offer an 11¼-inch tread. You can visually tie the steps to the deck if you use the same material for both treads and decking.

Both ends of each stringer must be firmly anchored either to a structure or to concrete footings. If the stairway is over 4 feet wide, add a third stringer down the center. For extremely wide steps, plan a stringer every 4 feet. (These calculations presume 1½-inch-thick lumber for treads.)

Measuring for stairs. To determine the number of steps you need, measure the vertical distance (total rise) from the deck to the ground; then divide by the riser height you intend to use. For example, if the deck is 45½ inches above grade and you plan on using 6½-inch risers, you need 7 steps exactly—45½ divided by 6½. If this formula gives you a number of steps ending in a fraction, divide the whole number into the vertical distance to learn the exact riser measurements. That is, if the deck is 54 inches above grade, 54 divided by 6½ inches per riser equals 8+ steps; 54 divided by 8 equals 6¾ inches rise per step.

Next, subtract twice the exact riser height from the maximum tread depth (26 inches) to find the proper depth of each tread. For a 6½-inch riser, the

Typical Tread-to-Riser Ratios

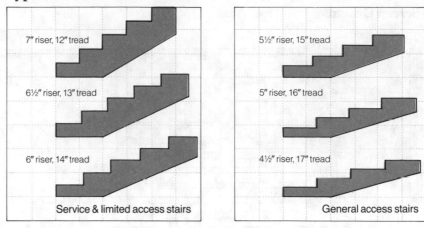

7″ riser, 12″ tread

6½″ riser, 13″ tread

6″ riser, 14″ tread

Service & limited access stairs

5½″ riser, 15″ tread

5″ riser, 16″ tread

4½″ riser, 17″ tread

General access stairs

For comfortable climbing, stair treads and risers should be designed according to ratios shown. More abrupt risers (see at left) are acceptable for limited access stairs.

proper tread depth is 13 inches— 26 minus 13.

Finally, determine the total run to find out whether your plan will fit the available space. Multiply the tread depth by the number of risers minus one: 7 steps with 13-inch-deep treads would have a run of 78 inches (13 times 6), for example. If the steps don't fit, adjust the riser-tread relationship, increasing one and decreasing the other.

Hand railings for stairs. Hand railings are seldom required for passage widths of 8 feet or more, even though the rise may be several feet. On the other hand, stairs and ramps with passage widths of 4 or 5 feet almost always need hand railings regardless of the rise height, for both safety and a feeling of security. Long ramps are also good candidates for hand railings.

Generally, hand railings on stairs and ramps must meet the same design requirements as the deck perimeter railings described on page 64. Measured from the top of the railing to the top front edges of the treads, the railing height must be at least 30 inches, at most 34 inches. Posts should be bolted or lag screwed to the stringers, never to the stair treads or ramp surface. Cap the tops of posts.

Ramps

Ramps are useful for deck access where the rise is less than 36 inches (the ramp's length may be a drawback for higher rises). Ramp passage widths are determined by the same general rules given for stairs on page 65.

A simple ramp is made from the same material as the deck supported by two or more 4 by 4 stringers, attached to deck joists, facers, or substructure members by the methods illustrated for stairs on the facing page.

The length of the ramp determines its slope. To find the shortest length for a comfortable walking slope, multiply the height of the rise by 8. You can always use a longer ramp, but a shorter one will be too steep for general access. One tip: Be sure to measure the rise from the ground (or patio or lower deck) to the top surface of the deck. To eliminate tripping, make sure all meeting surfaces are flush.

Changing Deck Levels

Decks are often built on several levels. In some cases, the second level is simply a narrow walkway; sometimes it's a landing, other times another surface. Methods for linking levels are shown on the facing page.

Stairs, Ramps & Level Changes

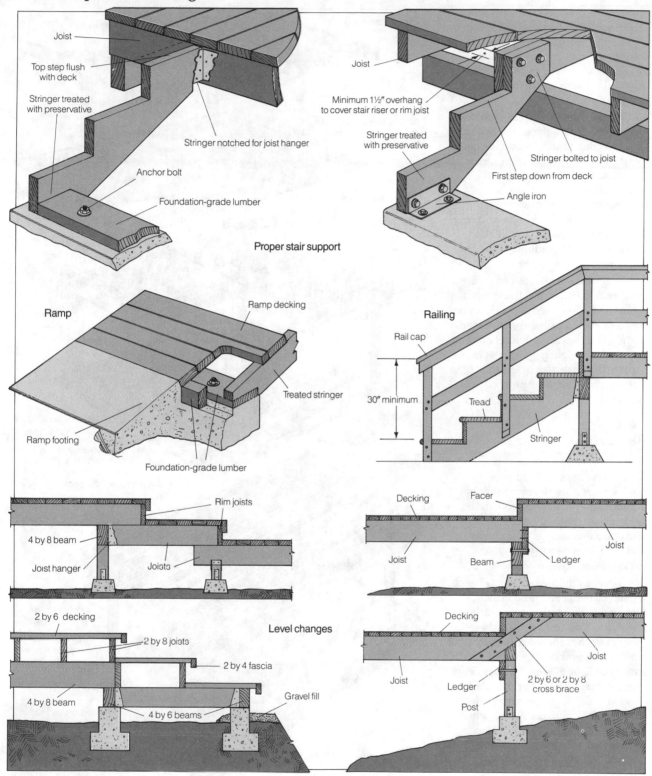

Joist

Top step flush with deck

Stringer treated with preservative

Stringer notched for joist hanger

Anchor bolt

Foundation-grade lumber

Joist

Minimum 1½" overhang to cover stair riser or rim joist

Stringer treated with preservative

Stringer bolted to joist

First step down from deck

Angle iron

Proper stair support

Ramp

Ramp decking

Treated stringer

Ramp footing

Foundation-grade lumber

Railing

Rail cap

30" minimum

Tread

Stringer

Rim joists

4 by 8 beam

Joist hanger

Joists

Decking

Facer

Joist

Joist

Beam

Ledger

Level changes

2 by 6 decking

2 by 8 joists

2 by 4 fascia

4 by 8 beam

4 by 6 beams

Gravel fill

Decking

Joist

Joist

Ledger

Post

2 by 6 or 2 by 8 cross brace

Stairs and ramps—and decks with changes in levels—are relatively easy to design and build. Provide sturdy support for stringers at both top and bottom.

OVERHEADS

Overheads filter light, provide protection from rain, and simply add to the intimacy and esthetics of a deck. Wood, plastic, glass, and fabrics are all possible materials for overhead construction.

An overhead's supporting framework is usually similar to a deck's substructure, but lighter; 30 pounds per square foot loading generally meets legal requirements in light-snowfall areas. Rafters are equivalent to joists; beams, ledgers, and posts serve the same purpose for both decks and overheads. Overheads are stronger if their posts are actually continuations of the deck's posts.

Build an overhead as you would a deck, remembering that the spans of beams and joists listed in the tables on pages 62–63 can usually be increased slightly (check with your local building department). Generally, it's best never to place the lowest beam less than 6 feet, 8 inches above the finished deck surface.

BENCHES

Benches serve as multipurpose outdoor furniture all year round. In addition, they can funnel foot traffic, separate areas for different activities, and double as railings for both low- and high-level decks (for high-level decks, use benches with backs).

For conventional seating, a bench should be between 15 and 18 inches high; sunbathing platforms may be as low as 6 to 8 inches. Backs on chair-height benches should offer support at least 12 inches above the seat; the seat itself should be at least 15 inches deep. Backs of built-in deck benches can be capped like railings; the caps protect the post ends from decay and, when level, provide surfaces to hold food and drinks.

Bench legs or supporting members should be sturdy enough to provide solid support, yet in scale with the bench design. Pairs of legs made

Overhead Designs

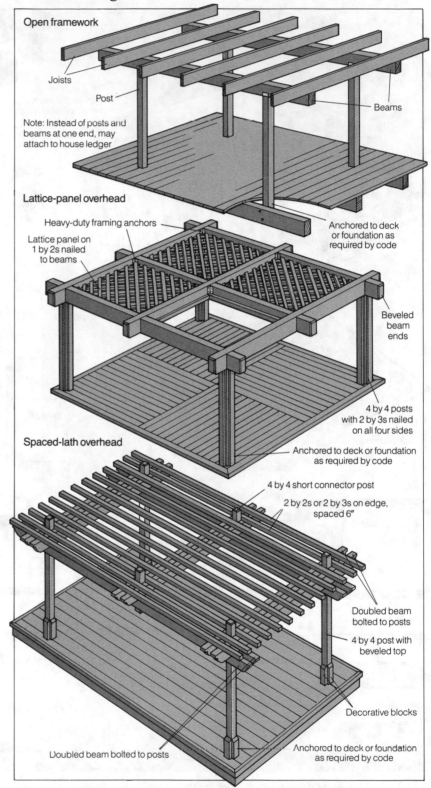

Open framework

Joists

Post

Beams

Note: Instead of posts and beams at one end, may attach to house ledger

Anchored to deck or foundation as required by code

Lattice-panel overhead

Heavy-duty framing anchors

Lattice panel on 1 by 2s nailed to beams

Beveled beam ends

4 by 4 posts with 2 by 3s nailed on all four sides

Anchored to deck or foundation as required by code

Spaced-lath overhead

4 by 4 short connector post

2 by 2s or 2 by 3s on edge, spaced 6"

Doubled beam bolted to posts

4 by 4 post with beveled top

Decorative blocks

Doubled beam bolted to posts

Anchored to deck or foundation as required by code

Overhead can be a simple, open framework or a more complex patio roof.

from 4 by 4s (or a material of similar strength) should be spaced 3 to 5 feet apart; if you're using 2 by 4s or other lightweight materials, or if the seat top needs additional support, the legs will be spaced more closely. Always choose surfaced lumber for seating.

OTHER AMENITIES

As you finalize your deck design, don't forget the amenities that can make a deck more functional and enjoyable—lighting, plumbing, planters, or trellises, for example.

On a raised deck, it's generally easier to run wiring and plumbing after the deck is finished. Your needs may be clearer once you've had a chance to use the deck a bit, too. But a low-level deck may require wiring or plumbing during construction of the substructure—and since permits may be needed, it pays to plan ahead. For more about deck amenities, see page 90.

You may also decide to incorporate special features such as hinged sections of decking (or bench tops) that lift up for storing hoses, outdoor equipment, or toys; such trapdoors may even conceal a sandbox. For additional deck storage ideas, see pages 43 and 91.

Bench Designs

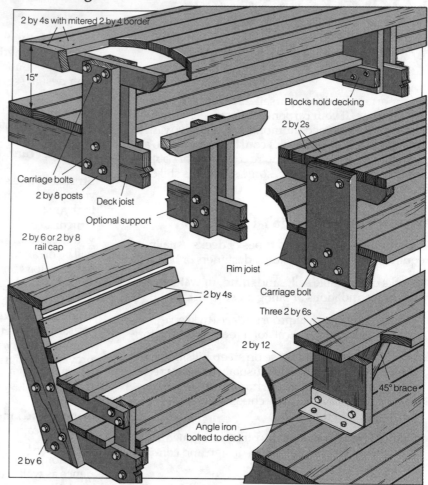

Benches are easiest to build if connected to deck's structure. Angled-back bench can double as a railing.

Deck Builder's Checklist

Here's a handy outline you can use to stay on track in your deck design and building process.

1) Choose site.

2) Gather ideas, sketches.

3) Draw or obtain base map.

4) Hire designer (optional).

5) Develop working drawings.

6) Estimate costs.

7) Finalize design.

8) Get permits.

9) Get contractor bids (optional).

10) Price materials.

11) Arrange financing, insurance if needed.

12) Select contractor (optional)

13) Purchase materials.

14) Begin construction.

15) Call for building inspections (if required).

16) Finish and enjoy!

WORKING WITH PROS

It's important for do-it-yourselfers to know where to draw the line. If your carpentry efforts seem to produce only a blackened thumbnail, you might want to consider turning your deck's construction over to a professional. And even if you're confident of your ability to build a basic deck, some situations still call for special design skills.

When to Hire a Professional

Certain site conditions and types of decks usually require the help of professional designers or builders.

■ Decks on unstable soil, sand, mud, or water need special foundations or piling for support.

■ Decks requiring a leakproof surface (to keep a below-deck room dry) call for a roofing contractor.

■ High-level decks and those on steep hillsides are difficult to build, since they usually involve special design methods. (Once the framework is in place, though, homeowners may choose to complete such a deck on their own.)

■ Cantilevered decks, usually built simultaneously with the house, call for special design and construction techniques.

■ Decks that end up including home remodeling— installing a door, wiring electrical outlets or lighting, or putting in plumbing—may require professional expertise.

Which Pro to Choose

Who is the right person to help you adapt, develop, or build your deck? Here are some of the professionals who can help you, along with a brief look at what they do.

Architects and landscape architects. These state-licensed professionals have a bachelor's or master's degree in architecture or landscape architecture. They're trained to create functional, structurally sound, esthetically pleasing designs; they also know the ins and outs of construction materials, understand the mechanics of estimating, and can negotiate bids from contractors and supervise the actual work.

Landscape and building designers. Landscape designers usually have a landscape architect's educa-

tion and training, but not a state license. Building designers, whether licensed (by the American Institute of Building Designers) or unlicensed, may offer design services along with construction.

Draftspersons. Drafters may be members of a skilled trade or unlicensed architects' apprentices. They can make the working drawings (from which you or your contractor can work) needed for building permits.

Structural and soils engineers. Before approving your plans, your building department may require that you (or your designer) consult with a soils or structural engineer under several circumstances: if you're planning a high-level deck, if the structure will be on an unstable or steep lot, or if strong winds or heavy loads might come into play.

Soils engineers evaluate soil conditions on a proposed construction site, then establish design specifications for foundations that can resist whatever stresses the soil might exert. Structural engineers, often working with the calculations a soils engineer provides, design foundation piers and footings to suit the site. They'll also calculate wind, seismic, and load stresses for the structure.

General and landscape contractors. Licensed general and landscape contractors specialize in construction (landscape contractors specialize in garden construction), though some have design skills and experience as well. They usually charge less for design work than landscape architects do, but their design skills may be limited by a construction point of view.

Contractors hired to build a small project may do all the work themselves; on a large project, they assume the responsibility for hiring qualified subcontractors, ordering construction materials, and seeing that the job is completed according to contract.

Subcontractors. If you act as your own general contractor, it's up to you to hire, coordinate, and supervise whatever subcontractors the job requires—specialists in carpentry, grading, plumbing, electrical work, and the like. You're not limited to working with subcontractors; you can hire workers with the necessary skills, but in that case, you'll be responsible for permits, insurance, and payroll taxes.

Aside from doing work according to the working drawings you provide, subcontractors can often supply you with current product information and sell hardware and supplies.

When dealing with subcontractors, give them clear instructions, put all firm agreements in writing, and provide as much direct supervision (of the sub-contractors, not their employees) as you can. Be sure you make it plain where one subcontractor's work ends and the next one's begins.

Finding & Selecting a Professional

When you're looking for design professionals or builders, friends and neighbors are often the best sources of information—most top-quality professionals gain much of their work by word-of-mouth from satisfied clients. Trade associations can also recommend licensed professionals in your area; check the Yellow Pages under "Associations" or "Labor Organizations." Of course, you can simply look up Yellow Page listings for the specific services you want.

Though some excellent professional designers have no professional affiliation, many belong to the American Society of Landscape Architects (ASLA), American Institute of Architects (AIA), American Institute of Building Designers (AIBD), or a state landscape contractors' association. To locate members in your area, contact a nearby office.

You can also look to the people who work with those whom you seek. Landscape architects can help you find contractors; material suppliers or subcontractors can refer you to contractors.

Before hiring a design professional, interview two or three; discuss the goals of your project. The right designer for you will be the one who is not only knowledgeable and competent, but also compatible with you and your family.

It's also wise to talk to several recommended contractors and get estimates from them. At this stage, you are under no obligation to hire a contractor. Don't automatically choose the contractor offering the lowest bid; base your decision on the individual's reputation as well (check his or her references). The contractor you hire should be well established, cooperative, competent, financially solvent (check bank and credit references), and insured for worker's compensation, property damage, and public liability.

Designer Procedures

If you include either an architect or landscape architect in your project, at least three working arrangements are open to you.

Retained on a consultation basis, an architect or landscape architect will review your plans, possibly suggest ideas for a more effective design, and perhaps provide a couple of rough conceptual sketches.

After that, it will be up to you to prepare the working drawings for the building department.

You also may hire a professional to design or modify your project and provide working drawings, with the understanding that you yourself will oversee the construction. For the design and working drawings, you may be charged either a flat fee or an hourly rate.

Finally, you can retain a landscape architect or architect on a planning-through-construction basis. Besides designing your project and providing working drawings and specifications, the architect will supervise the construction process. It will cost you more (usually 10 to 15 percent of the cost of the work) to have your project designed and built this way, but you will also be free from the plethora of details you'd have to handle otherwise.

The Building Contract

If you hire a contractor to build your deck, the more complete your plans and your contract, the better your chances that neither the process nor the result will be flawed. A solid contract should specify the items outlined below.

Construction materials. The contract should identify all construction materials by brand name, quality markings, and model numbers where applicable.

Work to be performed. All the work you expect the contractor to do should be clearly stated in the contract. For example, if you want the contractor to prepare the site, be sure you explicitly identify the appropriate tasks.

Time schedule. Though a contractor cannot be responsible for construction delays caused by strikes and material shortages, he or she should assume responsibility for completing the project within a reasonable period of time. Your best leverage is to stipulate that the final payment will be withheld until work is finished and the building department has granted final approval.

Method of payment. Construction is usually paid for in one of two ways. You can either make one payment at the beginning of the project and a second upon completion, or pay in installments as work progresses. The installment plan, though sometimes confusing, generally works better for the homeowner, since it's in your best interest to minimize the amount you pay before seeing actual progress.

EASY DECK PLANS

Studying actual deck designs is perhaps the best way to understand how the various structural elements interrelate. Here and on the facing page, we show plans for two of the most common deck types: a simple single-level deck and a slightly more complex two-level deck.

Besides using these plans to study construction, you can actually build from them—either directly (if site and codes permit) or by adapting them to suit your particular situation.

LOW-LEVEL DECK

A low-level deck like this one can transform any unused part of your yard into a flat, comfortable "outdoor floor" that's ideal for almost any outdoor activity, from sunbathing to picnicking. Because this deck is so small (just 8 by 12 feet), it will fit in even a postage-stamp–sized yard. Its construction is simple, but illustrates all the basic components of most freestanding, low-level decks.

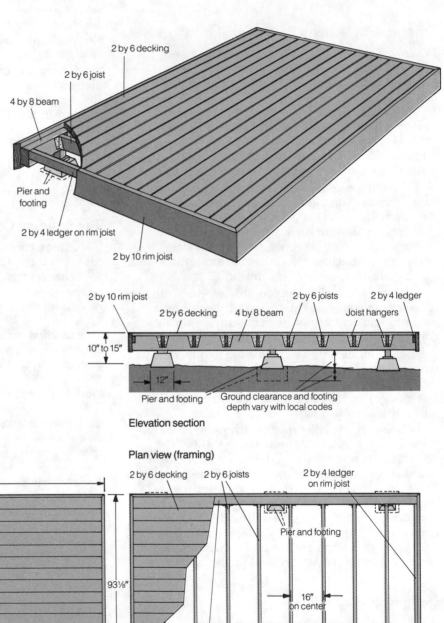

2 by 6 decking

2 by 6 joist

4 by 8 beam

Pier and footing

2 by 4 ledger on rim joist

2 by 10 rim joist

2 by 10 rim joist 2 by 6 decking 4 by 8 beam 2 by 6 joists 2 by 4 ledger Joist hangers

10" to 15"

12"

Pier and footing Ground clearance and footing depth vary with local codes

Elevation section

Plan view (decking)

12'

93⅛"

Plan view (framing)

2 by 6 decking 2 by 6 joists 2 by 4 ledger on rim joist

Pier and footing

16" on center

4 by 8 beams Joist hangers

TWO-LEVEL DECK

Decks built on a slope often step down to hug the terrain. This one, which can be built either freestanding or attached to a house ledger, has a single level change. Look closely at the beam and joist configurations to see how a drop in level is typically handled; if you'd like to design a deck with several level changes, just replicate these methods.

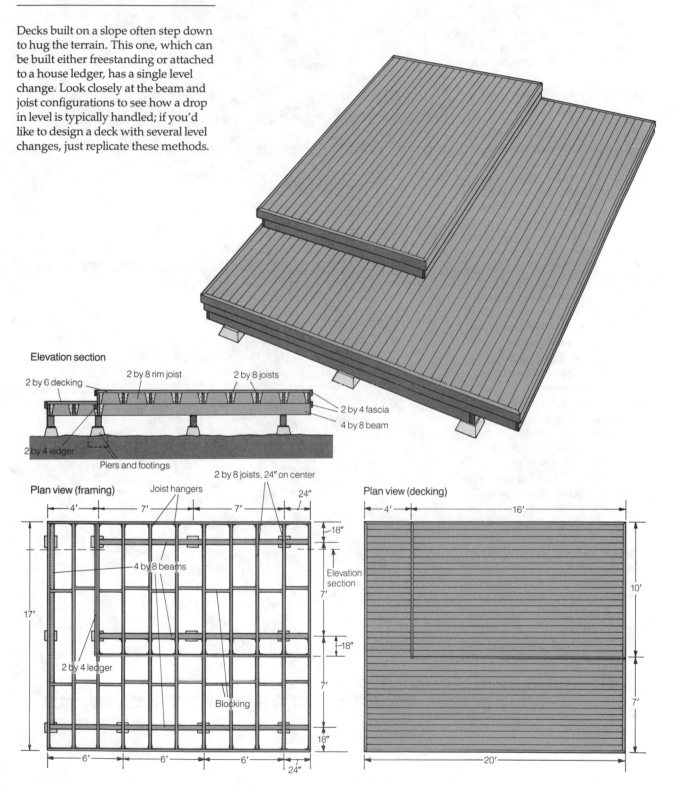

Elevation section

2 by 6 decking
2 by 8 rim joist
2 by 8 joists
2 by 4 fascia
4 by 8 beam
2 by 4 ledger
Piers and footings

Plan view (framing)

2 by 8 joists, 24" on center
Joist hangers
24"
4'
7'
7'
18"
Elevation section
4 by 8 beams
7'
17'
18"
2 by 4 ledger
7'
Blocking
18"
6'
6'
6'
24"

Plan view (decking)

4'
16'
18"
10'
Elevation section
7'
7'
20'

SPECIAL SITUATIONS

Most decks conform to basic frame-style construction, with substructures of joists, beams, posts, and so forth. But some decks—specifically those laid on patio surfaces and rooftops—are built slightly differently. Here's a closer look.

DECKING OVER A PATIO

If you have a damaged or unsightly patio, perhaps the easiest and least expensive way to update it is to cover it with a new deck. As long as you use approved materials and practices, most codes will allow a simple, low-level deck to be laid directly on a patio. Support for the decking is provided by foundation-grade sleepers—typically 2 by 4s laid flat—fastened directly to the concrete.

To ensure decay resistance, the sleepers are always made from either pressure-treated lumber or redwood, cedar, or cypress heartwood.

If you want to run your deck beyond the perimeter of the patio slab, part of it will take on more standard deck construction: the sleepers must be scaled up to 4 by 4s and supported by a typical arrangement of foundations, posts, and beams as shown in the bottom drawing at right.

For 2 by 4 or 2 by 6 decking, plan to place 2 by 4 sleepers on 24-inch centers. If your patio isn't level or if it's cracked and irregular, shim the sleepers with small redwood wedges or cedar shingles. And if the patio is sloped for runoff, be sure to run the sleepers in the direction of the slope, so water won't pool behind them.

You can fasten sleepers by gluing them with exterior construction adhesive or by "shooting" them down with a power hammer, a gunlike device that blasts concrete nails into the concrete (available from tool rental centers). If you use adhesive, run a bead along the part of the sleepers' lengths that will contact the slab.

Fasten decking to sleepers just as you would attach decking to joists (see page 87).

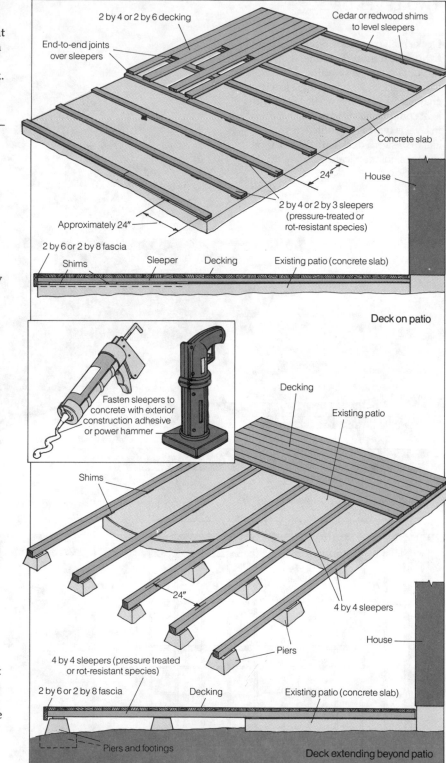

Decking rests on sleepers fastened to concrete patio surface.

DECKING ON A ROOF

Rooftop decks take advantage of the wasted space on house and garage roofs, turning an unused area into a pleasant place to enjoy views, sun, and breezes.

You can build your deck right on top of the roof—an especially easy route to follow if the roof is flat. You can also remove portions of the roof and/or side walls and create a deck adjacent to an existing room; an attached garage or single-story wing may already be waiting to give you this kind of opportunity.

If your deck is above the house, you'll need a stairway or ladder for access. Check local codes for requirements regarding stairs.

Because a roof deck places additional loads on your house roof, walls, and foundation, you'll need to consult an architect or engineer to see if reinforcing framing is required.

For a flat or slightly pitched surface, a conventional built-up roof of felt and hot-mopped asphalt is the most common waterproofer, but it's not a traffic surface itself; you'll need to put decking of some kind on top of it. Wood decking laid over such a roof is usually supported by sleeper boards set on their sides. The idea is to spread the total load over a wide area, thus reducing the point load as much as possible.

To avoid penetrating the roofing material with nails or screws, build modular, interlocking decking sections that rest on 2 by 4 sleepers made from pressure-treated lumber or redwood, cedar, or cypress heartwood as shown at right. If you make these sections 4 feet square, they can easily be removed for roof cleaning or repair. Be sure roof drainage isn't obstructed; if necessary, cut or drill drainage holes in the sleepers. (Refer to page 87 for information on attaching decking.)

The drawing also shows rooftop decks surfaced with pavers, single-ply bitumen roofing, and tile.

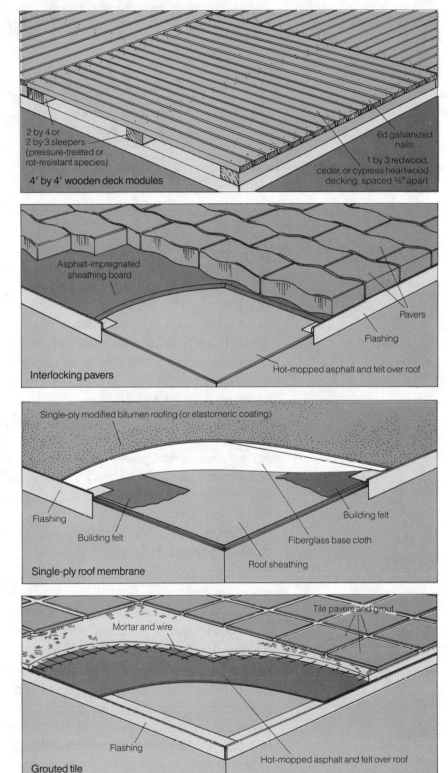

Rooftop decks can be surfaced with a variety of materials.

BUILDING YOUR DECK

When you're ready to strap on your tool belt, consider this chapter your guide to proven deck-building techniques. But before forging ahead, remember that, though some decks are relatively easy to build, others are best left to an experienced builder. If you're new to construction, stick to simple, low-level designs.

Allow plenty of time for your project—you'll have to prepare the site; lay out the foundation; erect posts, beams, and joists; put down the decking; add any amenities; and apply a finish. Of course, you won't always perform these tasks in exactly the order given, and some jobs may need to be done at several different stages.

If your plan includes stairs, overheads, or other amenities, note that their supports are often best connected to the substructure during assembly, not after completion.

The basic tools you'll need include a utility knife, tape measure, level, plumb bob, mason's line, chalk line, combination and framing squares, shovel, handsaw, power circular saw, power drill, hammer, nailset, flat pry bar, wrench, caulking gun, safety goggles, gloves, and paintbrush.

PREPARING THE SITE

To make sure the building process goes smoothly, start by taking care of some initial site preparation. Now is the time to solve drainage problems, handle any necessary grading, and nip future weed growth in the bud.

Drainage. Though a deck can span low spots too boggy for use, the soil supporting it must be firm: you don't want it to sink during the first heavy rain. A proper drainage system should carry water away from the house and the deck's substructure, particularly the footings.

A drainage ditch dug in the direction of the runoff is generally best for diverting unwanted water. Dig it at least 1 foot deep, with a minimum slope of 1 inch for every 15 feet of distance. Shovel a 1-inch layer of gravel along the base of the trench, then lay 4-inch perforated plastic drainpipe on top with the holes facing *downward*. Cover the pipe with 8 inches of gravel, then fill the ditch with dirt to grade level. (Where runoff is slight, a ditch filled with gravel alone is sufficient.)

Concrete trough carries heavy runoff.

On a hillside site, your concern won't be so much getting rid of standing water as channeling surface runoff to minimize erosion. To take care of this job, you can install a concrete trough or spillway running downhill from a collection point. If runoff is heavy, build the trough with a flare at the downhill end to make the water flow more slowly and spread it over a wider area (planted to hold soil). In extreme cases, an outfall of large rocks may be needed to prevent erosion.

Grading. Though decks typically bridge across a yard's bumps and dips, it may be necessary to knock down a high spot or two to control a deck's height. In most situations, this is just a matter of shifting dirt from a higher area to a lower one. Remember that the spots where footings will go shouldn't be filled, since loose soil needs careful repacking to support footings.

Weed control. Most low-level decks naturally prohibit weed growth by blocking out the light and air the plants need to grow. Nonetheless, it's wise to cover the ground with black 6- to 10-mil polyethylene sheeting or treat the soil with weed killer just before you lay the decking across the substructure.

How to Create a Drainage Ditch

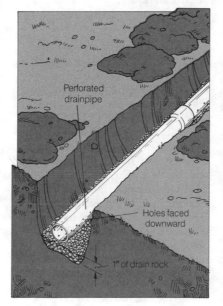

Dig trench toward runoff, sloping it at least 1 inch for every 15 feet.

Shovel a 1-inch bed of gravel into trench; lay perforated pipe on top.

Cover pipe with at least 8 inches of gravel; fill to grade level with dirt.

MOUNTING A LEDGER

As discussed on page 60, a ledger connects a deck to a house or some other structure.

Placing the ledger. Bolts or lag screws securing a ledger to a wood-frame house wall must go through exterior siding into solid interior framing members, ideally floor joists.

When you determine a ledger's height outside a door, allow for the decking's thickness and, if joists will rest on top of the ledger, the joist height. Also be sure to drop the deck's surface ½ to 1 inch below interior floor level to keep water out. Take care to mount the ledger level.

Fastening a ledger to wood-frame house walls. Nails alone are *never* sufficient for securing a ledger. On walls of wood-frame (including stuccoed) houses, first nail or brace the ledger in place. Then, if you can get under the house floor to add washers and nuts, drill and fasten the ledger with carriage bolts. Otherwise, drill lag screw pilot holes through the ledger and siding into the house's framing (use a masonry bit to drill stucco). You'll need to set two ½- or ⅝-inch-diameter lag screws at each end of the ledger and stagger the rest up and down every 16 inches.

Remove the ledger, slip a washer onto each lag screw, then run the screws into the ledger until the points protrude about ½ inch. The lag screws you use should be long enough to penetrate the framing to a minimum of 3 inches, or as specified by local codes.

For moisture protection, pack each pilot hole in the house wall with silicone caulk. As a further guard against water damage (unless you plan to flash the ledger, as described at right), slip three or four large washers onto the end of each lag screw as spacers between the house wall and ledger. Position the ledger and drive in the lag screws.

Fastening a ledger to masonry house walls or foundations. To anchor a ledger to a masonry wall,

Ledger Attachment Techniques

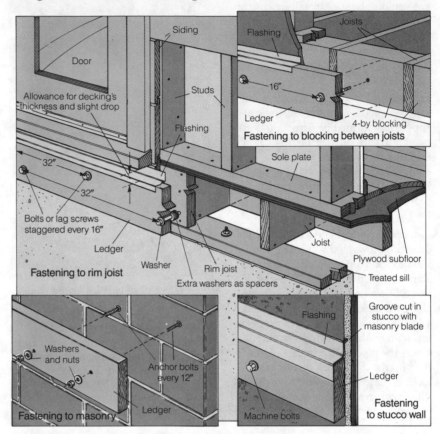

Because a ledger bears a heavy load, it must be solidly attached to house's structure.

use expanding anchor bolts. Mark a line across the wall for the ledger's top edge, drill holes for expanding anchors (see drawing above), and insert the anchors.

If you have a helper, hold the ledger in place and tap it with a hammer to indent the anchor locations on the back face. Then remove the ledger and drill bolt holes through it at the marks made by the bolt tips. If you're working by yourself, just measure and transfer the bolt locations to the ledger. Push (or hammer) the ledger onto the bolts; recheck the level and make any necessary adjustments, add washers and nuts, and tighten.

Flashing the ledger. To keep moisture from penetrating into the space between ledger and house wall, it's a good idea to flash a ledger before you fasten the joists in place. You can use either ready-made aluminum or galvanized sheet metal Z-flashing.

Fit the flashing and caulk the top edge. Then nail the top with galvanized nails long enough to penetrate at least 1 inch into wall studs or other structural members. (To fasten flashing to brick or concrete, use short masonry nails.) Daub the nail heads with caulking compound.

If the house is sided with shingles or lap siding, don't caulk the flashing's top edge; instead, slip the flashing up under the bottom edge of shingles or siding. For a stucco wall, fit the crimped top edge of the flashing into a groove cut with a masonry saw blade.

LAYING OUT THE FOUNDATION

For proper support, most decks require a foundation—normally a series of concrete piers and footings. (Rooftop decks and those built directly on top of concrete patios are exceptions; see pages 74 and 75 for more information.) Because each pier holds a post (or a beam), pier placement is governed by post locations, which are in turn determined by beam and joist spans. You will have worked out all the relevant measurements during the design stage (see pages 58–63); now you can simply transfer them to the ground.

A rectangular or square deck should have corners that are truly square—at 90° angles. And if your deck is house-attached, its sides should be perpendicular to the house wall. To be sure you lay out the corners square, use the 3-4-5 rule. This triangulation method works in any multiple of 3-4-5, such as 6-8-10 (as shown), 9-12-15, or even 12-16-20. For maximum accuracy, use the largest multiple possible.

To carry out the procedure, you'll need a helper and two tape measures. On a house-attached deck, begin by driving two nails into the ledger: one

at the end, the other exactly 6 feet away. Have your helper hook the end of a tape measure onto each nail. Then pull out the tapes until the 8-foot mark on the tape attached to the ledger's end intersects the 10-foot mark on the other tape, as shown below left. Drive a stake into the ground at this point. From the ledger's end and in line with the stake, measure the proper distance from the house for the corner pier and drive in a stake to mark that spot. Repeat on the other side to locate the other corner pier.

For a freestanding deck, use the same technique to maintain 90° corners; just work from stakes pounded into the ground instead of nails driven into a ledger.

String lines from ledger to corner. Using these lines as your guide, transfer the remaining pier locations to the ground, using a tape measure and level or plumb bob (see drawing below center). Mark footing holes with white lime, or just cut in a portion of each hole with a shovel. Dig holes, sized as required by your codes (see page 55). It's a good idea to dig deep enough to allow for about 6 inches of gravel beneath concrete. Before adding

the gravel, tamp the bottom of each hole and add any necessary steel reinforcing bars (normally required if piers are over a foot high or if only a few are used).

In preparation for pouring footings and placing piers or post anchors, set up batterboards as shown below right. These will help you adjust and maintain taut, exact perimeter lines for placing post anchors. Locate batterboards about 18 inches from each corner stake.

Run mason's lines from each end of the ledger (or corner stakes) to the opposite batterboards, then from batterboard to batterboard, as shown in the illustration. To check for square, measure the diagonal distance between opposite corners; adjust the lines until the distances between the two sets of corners are equal.

With a level or plumb bob, plumb down from the intersections of the mason's lines to recheck the locations of the corner piers.

Remember that these lines mark the posts' outer faces, not their centers. Be sure to make the necessary allowances when you're centering the footings.

How to Lay Out Footings

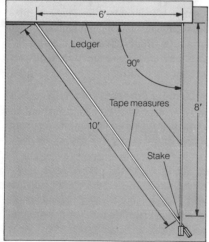

Establish true square by creating a 3-4-5 triangle with two tape measures.

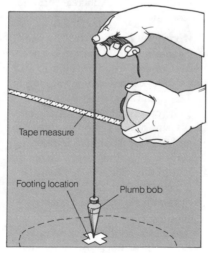

Measure out from wall along line; plumb down for pier locations.

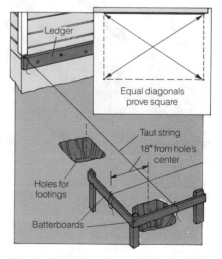

Dig footing holes. Set up batterboards to refine layout for piers.

POURING THE FOUNDATION

If your deck's foundation will require much hand-mixing or pouring of concrete, be prepared for a day of hard work and a night of sound sleep. There's nothing like working with concrete to test your stamina.

Premixed concrete. For a relatively small job, you can buy dry ready-mix concrete that requires only the addition of water before it's ready to pour. Such premixed concrete is slightly more expensive but immensely more convenient than making up your own concrete from sand, gravel, and cement. As a rule of thumb, one 90-pound sack of premixed concrete will pour one 12- by 12- by 8-inch footing.

Mixing concrete from bulk materials. Though premixed concrete can make life easier, it pays to mix your own if you need a fairly large quantity. Use 1 part cement, 2 parts clean river sand, and 3 parts gravel (1-inch diameter maximum, specially washed for concrete mixing). Add clean water, a little at a time, as you mix. To get the right con-

Typical Foundations

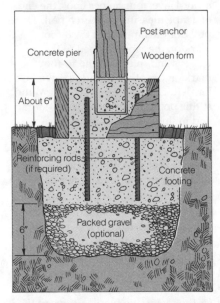

Pier and footing may be formed and poured together.

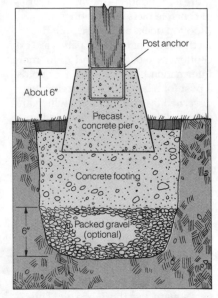

Easiest foundation is made by setting a precast pier in a poured footing.

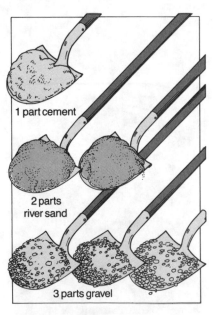

Concrete-mixing formula calls for these proportions of cement, sand, and gravel.

sistency—plastic, but not runny—it's important to get the proper ratio of water to cement. The mixture of water and powderlike cement forms an adhesive that binds the sand and gravel, causing the concrete to harden. Adding too much water thins or dilutes this adhesive paste and weakens its cementing ability; adding too little makes the concrete stiff and unworkable.

■ *Mixing by hand.* To mix by hand, you can put the materials in a wheelbarrow or on a wooden platform and use a shovel or hoe as your mixing tool. Spread two shovelfuls of sand and one of cement on the mixing surface. Using a rolling motion, mix these ingredients until the color is even. Add three shovelfuls of gravel; again, mix until the color is even. Finally, scoop out a hole in the middle of the dry ingredients and add 3 quarts of water.

Work around the edges of the puddle with a shovel or a hoe, slowly rolling the dry ingredients into the water. Take particular care not to slop

the water out of the wheelbarrow (or off the platform), since escaping water may weaken the batch by carrying particles of cement with it.

If the batch is too stiff, add more water, about 1 cup at a time, mixing until the texture is right. If the mixture is too soupy, add small amounts of sand and gravel (keep to the proper ratio—2 parts sand, 3 parts gravel). Bear in mind that at this stage of mixing, the addition of even small amounts of ingredients can change the concrete's consistency radically, so measure carefully.

■ *Using a powered mixer.* To make your work easier, you might consider renting a powered cement mixer from a tool rental outlet.

To mix in a machine-powered mixer, estimate the proportions of cement, sand, and gravel by shovelfuls; add 2½ gallons of water per half-bag of cement. Tumble for 2 or 3 minutes, then pour.

To form piers. It is far easier to buy precast concrete piers to set in poured

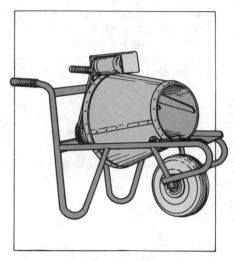

This unusual powered cement mixer doubles as a wheelbarrow.

concrete footings. But if you choose to make your own piers, here's how.

Scrap lumber and plywood both make excellent forms; simply nail at the corners. (For large piers, you'll need to reinforce the forms with supports, such as lengths of wire twisted around the perimeter.) You can also buy specially manufactured cylindrical fiber forms that can be sawed to any desired length; they have a coated inner surface that makes them easy to peel off the cured concrete.

To pour footings and piers together. First pour all the footings to the depth and size required by local codes. Wait a few minutes, then place and level the piers' forms over the wet concrete footings, inserting any steel reinforcing rods, if required, to strengthen the link between footings and piers.

Fill the pier forms with concrete; use a screed or straight board to level the wet concrete flush with the tops of the forms. Immediately embed metal post anchors (see page 49) in the wet concrete piers. While the concrete is still plastic, hold a carpenter's level against a short length of post material placed in the post anchors to check for plumb.

Leave the forms on the new piers and keep them damp for at least a week while the concrete cures. To protect curing piers from direct sun or hot, dry weather, cover with newspapers, straw, or burlap sacks; keep covering moist so piers will dry slowly.

To place precast piers on wet concrete footings. Soak the piers with a hose. Pour the footings, wait a few minutes—until the wet concrete is able to support the piers—then position the piers and level them in both directions.

A post connected to a wooden nailing block on top of a precast pier won't be as secure as one fastened to a metal post anchor. Wooden blocks are fine for low-level decks, but for medium-height or tall decks, opt for metal post anchors.

To bond precast piers to dry footings. First drench the top of each footing and the bottom of each pier with water. Then coat both surfaces ½ to 1 inch thick with a creamy paste of cement; set the pier in place on the footing, checking to be sure the top of the pier is level.

How to Pour a Footing for a Precast Pier

Mix proper proportions of cement, sand, and gravel with water.

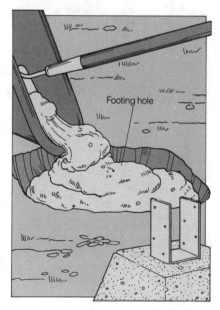

Pour concrete into footing hole, then soak precast pier with water.

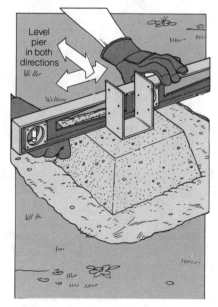

Allow concrete to set up a few minutes, then level pier in concrete.

ERECTING POSTS & BEAMS

Once the concrete footings start to cure, you can begin erecting posts and beams. The following directions assume a standard beam-on-post configuration; if a post will be sandwiched by a double beam or the beam will rest directly on a pier, you must modify the instructions accordingly.

If you are building a deck with railings, benches, overheads, and so forth, consider the extended-post assemblies discussed and illustrated on page 60.

Measuring & Cutting Posts

For a stable, level substructure, you must measure posts accurately and cut them squarely. If your deck is house-attached, work on the posts farthest from the house first. For a freestanding deck, begin with the posts supporting opposite edges and corners; then do any intermediate posts.

The methods for measuring posts for freestanding versus house-attached decks differ in only one respect: an attached deck's height is defined at the ledger line along the wall, while for freestanding decks, you work from a post at the deck's approximate height.

For a deck that must slope slightly for surface drainage, drop the otherwise level marks away from the house about 1 inch for every 10 feet.

As shown in the illustrations below, cut a post 6 to 12 inches longer than the estimated finish length. Have a helper hold the post firmly in place on its anchor; then plumb it, using a carpenter's level (check two adjacent sides). Stretch a string fitted with a line level from where the joists' bottom edges will connect to the ledger. When the string is level, mark the post as shown. (If you don't have a line level, use a carpenter's level and a straight length of lumber.)

From the mark on the post, subtract the actual thickness of any beam that will sit between the post and joists. Make a new mark and, with a combination square, carry it around the post's perimeter. This is your cutting line. Repeat for remaining posts.

Take each post down to cut it. Soak one raw end of each post (the end that will contact a pier) in wood preservative (see page 94). If you're using metal post caps, attach them to the posts' tops before raising the posts into position.

Setting Posts

Before moving the first post into position, drive stakes into the ground, then nail a brace made from a 1 by 2 or 1 by 3 to each stake (to allow the brace to pivot, use only one nail). Place the stakes where you won't have any trouble nailing the braces to the post sides once the post is in place, and set them far enough from the end of the post to allow the braces to reach

How to Mark a Post for Cutting

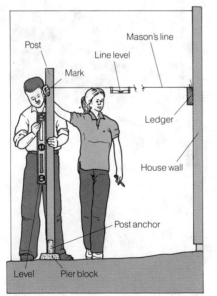

Position and plumb post, using a carpenter's level. Stretch a string to it, level with ledger, and mark post.

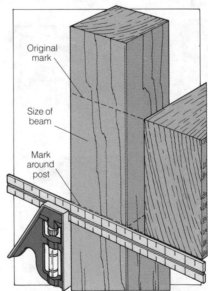

Subtract actual thickness of any beam that sits on posts. Mark around post with a combination square.

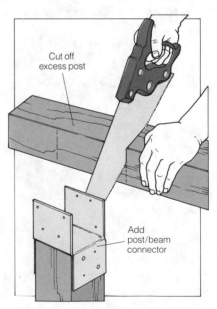

Take post down and cut end. Add post cap to top of post before re-erecting.

midway up the post at a 45° angle (be sure you cut the braces long enough).

Seat the post squarely in its anchor and check for plumb, using a carpenter's level on adjacent sides. Nail the braces to the post, keeping the post plumb. Then nail or lag-screw the post to its anchor. Finally, drive additional nails into each brace to secure the posts until the beams are seated.

Building Up Beams

A typical built-up beam consists of 2-by lumber, nailed together with 20d nails spaced 3 inches apart along the top and bottom edges and staggered in the central area; some built-up beams are bolted or lag-screwed.

If you must make a long beam from shorter lengths, stagger the end joints; each joint should occur over a post. Sight along each piece to find the crown (slight outward curve along the edge); align the crowns on the same side. When you mount the beam on the posts, place the crown side up unless the beam is cantilevered at one or both ends, in which case the crown side should face down.

If you must join two beams end to end, be sure the joint falls over a post. Splice with cleats ("gusset plates") of 2-by material or metal straps nailed to each face (see illustration on page 85).

Seating Beams

Beams that sit directly on piers are easy to attach: you can toenail them to the piers' nailing blocks or lag-screw them to metal anchors. Raising heavy beams onto fairly tall posts is another story, though.

To seat a heavy beam, drag it into rough position alongside the posts and slip a short length of 2 by 4 under one of its ends. Using the 2 by 4 to lift from both sides, have a helper assist you to raise that end of the beam, ma-neuvering it into the post cap (or a pair of wooden cleats nailed to the post's top). Temporarily nail the beam with one nail, then lift and place the other end.

Bolts with washers and nuts are the sturdiest fasteners. Drill through holes in the metal connector and then through the beam in one pass, using an extra-long drill bit or a bit with a shaft extension; or drill each hole from both sides.

Bracing Posts

Cross brace posts of decks taller than 3 feet before adding additional weight. Mark individual cross braces in position, then cut them on the ground; to save time later, pretreat the braces with wood finish. Temporarily nail them in place, drill pilot holes for bolts or lag screws, squirt the holes with wood finish, and permanently fasten with bolts or lag screws.

How to Set & Brace a Post

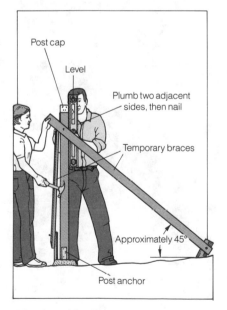

Plumb and brace post with temporary supports staked to ground. Fasten to post anchor.

Cradling it on a 2 by 4, hoist beam onto post cap. Temporarily nail that end, lift other end, and then bolt.

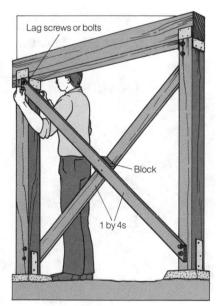

To add lateral stability on decks taller than 3 feet, cross brace posts. For other methods of bracing, see page 61.

LAYING OUT & FASTENING JOISTS

Once you've dealt with posts and beams, you're ready to lay out joist placements and secure the joists to the beams and the ledger (if there is one).

Marking Joist Layout

Starting at an outside corner, mark the 1½-inch thickness of the first joist, or stringer, with a line and an X. For standard 16-inch joist centers, hook your tape measure over the ledger's (or beam's) end and measure off 15¼ and 16¾ inches; mark lines at these points and put an X between them. From this pair of lines, continue to measure and mark in 16-inch intervals to the far end of the ledger.

Plan to double up joists around deck openings. When doing this, mark another line to one side, but don't disturb the basic 16-inch spacing. The last interval may be less than 16 inches.

Once the layout is complete, transfer the same spacing to the opposite beam, using a length of scrap lumber, as shown. (One exception: If you're splicing joists by overlapping them, as described at right, the layout on the opposite beam must be offset 1½ inches to allow for the overlap. Mark the outline of the first joist at 13¾ and 15¼ inches from the end; then mark every 16 inches, as before.)

Installing Joists

Choose the straightest, driest lumber you can find for floor joists. Sighting along each joist, find the crown and mark that side. Plan to install joists crown side up.

If you're mounting the joists in metal joist hangers, it saves time to get all the hangers in place before mounting any of the joists: just position and nail one side of each hanger to the ledger and beam. Then measure the distance between opposite (matching) hangers at each end and midway across the deck to see if joist lengths will be consistent. Joists mounted in these hangers can be up to ½ inch short of the proper measurement and still fit. If you find greater discrepancies in length, you'll have to measure and cut each joist individually; otherwise, cut all joists to length.

If you're nailing joists directly to the ledger's face, first nail blocking in place in alternate bays, as shown on facing page below left. This allows you to face-nail one side of the joists, then toenail the other (see "Blocking Joists" on the facing page).

A helper can speed up and streamline the job of positioning joists over 8 feet long. The secret is to set up a system that allows you and your helper to work in tandem, fastening both ends of each joist simultaneously. Together, lift and set each joist in its hanger; nail the other side of the hanger to the ledger or beam, then to the joist. After all the joists are in place, just nail a rim joist to their ends, using three or four 16d galvanized nails per joist (you'll only do this on joists that sit on top of beams).

Splicing Joists

Where looks aren't important, joists (and beams) can be spliced together from end to end. Use any of the methods illustrated on the facing page.

A splice must be supported by a beam or post. Be sure each joist end bears a full inch on the supporting

How to Lay Out Joist Locations

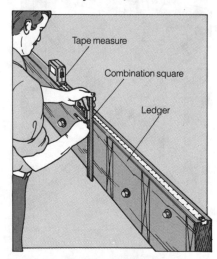

Measure and mark joist locations on ledger (or beam), using a combination square as a guide.

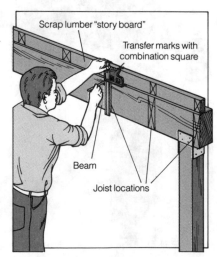

Transfer joist locations to other beams, using a "story board" of scrap lumber and a combination square.

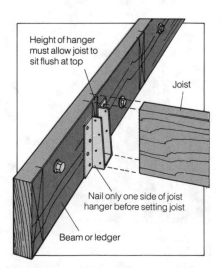

Nail one side of joist hanger to ledger (or beam) so that joist's top edge will sit flush with ledger's top edge.

member. If several spliced joists are needed, plan to stagger the splices over different beams to avoid weakening the substructure.

The overlap method of splicing is the easiest, but it breaks up uniform spacing—making your work harder later. If you use this method and more than one splice is needed on a full joist length, alternate overlapped sides. For standard 2-by lumber, nail both faces of each splice with six 8d or 10d galvanized common nails. Fasten other splice connections as illustrated at right.

Blocking Joists

Locations and requirements for blocking are discussed on pages 60–61. Snap a chalk line across joists at the relevant points; then work your way across the joists, measuring and listing the lengths of blocking you'll need to cut from the joist material. Cut and code blocks to correspond to their locations.

It's easiest to alternate the blocks, staggering them from one side of the chalk line to the other. By using this technique, you'll be able to end-nail the blocks instead of toenailing them.

How to Splice Joists & Beams

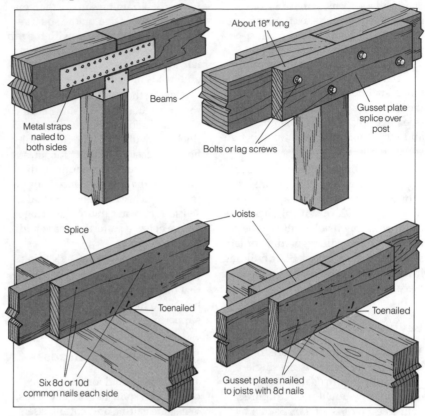

Splice together joists or beams over support members.

How to Install Joists

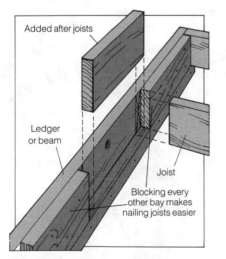

For nailing directly to ledger, first install blocking in every other between-joist space.

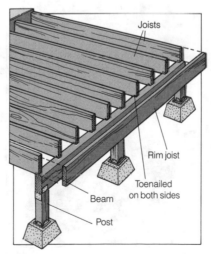

Nail all joists in place. For joists that sit on top of a beam, add a rim joist, nailing it to joist ends.

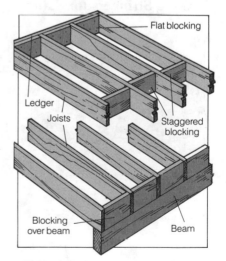

Add blocking between joists; staggered blocking is easiest to nail in place.

STAIRS & OTHER STRUCTURES

Most decks with railings, benches, overheads, screens, stairs, and/or ramps have supports for these amenities tied to the substructure. All supports that must be bolted or lag-screwed to the substructure should be secured before the decking is laid. Before installing such supports, review the information on protective finishes (see page 95); to make finishing easier and more thorough, treat wood before you assemble it.

Methods of bolting and interlocking supports to the substructure are shown in the planning chapter beginning on page 52. In general, these procedures simply involve cutting the members, then nailing, bolting, or lag-screwing them together. Stair building involves some extra tricks, though. Here are a few tips.

Laying Out Stringers

The strongest—and therefore the best—stringer design is the single-piece stringer with "sawtooth" cutouts for steps. You'll need knot-free, split-free 2 by 14s (or 4 by 8s or 4 by 10s) long enough to reach from the top landing to the bottom surface.

Mark the riser dimension on the tongue of a framing square; then mark the tread dimension on the square's body. Line up the marks with the top edge of the stringer, as shown below left, and trace the outline of the risers and treads onto it.

Cut out the notches with a handsaw or circular saw, finishing each cut with the handsaw. Because the tread thickness will add to the first step's height, measure the exact thickness of a tread and cut this amount off the bottom of the stringer. Once your pattern is cut, check the alignment; if it's satisfactory, you can use the stringer you've cut as a pattern to mark additional stringers.

Bolt the stringer to the deck's joists, to a beam, or to the ledger. Make sure that the stringers are secured at the bottom to the foundation or other supporting surface.

Adding Risers & Treads

Though most outdoor stairs have open risers, some have riser boards. When measuring and cutting risers and treads, remember that the bottom edge of a riser tucks behind the back

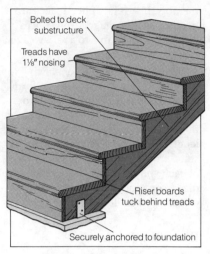

On closed riser stairs, nail risers in place before treads.

of the tread, and the forward edge of the tread overlaps the riser below it. Giving each tread a 1⅛-inch nosing (a projection beyond the front of the riser) lends a more finished appearance to the stairway you build.

Nail risers to the stringers first, then nail the treads to the stringers. Finally, fasten the bottom edges of the risers to the backs of the treads.

Making Stringers for Stairs

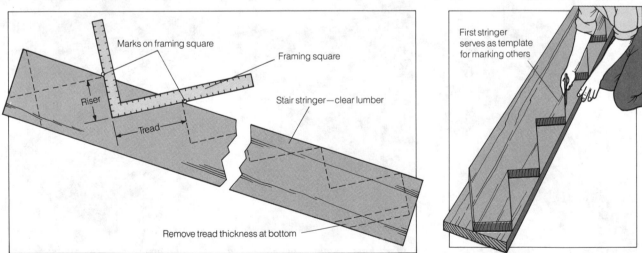

Lay out tread and riser dimensions on a stringer, using a framing square. Be sure to subtract tread thickness at bottom end. Cut stringer; then use it as a pattern for marking its mates.

LAYING THE DECKING

A deck's surface is not only the most visible part of a deck—it's often the easiest to build. Laying the decking usually involves simply measuring, cutting, and nailing, but knowing a few tricks of the trade will help you achieve a quality job.

Laying watertight decking is another story: specialized techniques not covered in this book are usually required to set down tile, concrete, fiberglass, and the materials needed beneath them. (For more about roof decks, refer to page 75.) Even so, you can prepare the deck for these materials by laying a plywood subfloor as explained on page 89. For information on various decking materials, see page 46 and pages 50–51.

LAYING WOOD DECKING

Before you lay the decking, take care of any remaining work on the substructure. If you intend to apply a protective finish to the substructure, do it now (see page 95)—and while you're at it, consider staining or treating your decking lumber before installation. This is also the time to install any plumbing or wiring on a low-level deck (see pages 90–91).

Both ends of every length of decking must be supported by a joist or beam. If the decking won't reach across the deck's full length, butt-join the pieces over joists, staggering the joints so that no two line up side by side over the same joist. To support ends of decking, add extra joist blocking around trees or anything else that penetrates the deck's surface.

If the appearance of the lumber permits, lay the boards bark side up to minimize checking and cupping. The bark side is the convex side of the board (the outer side of the tree's growth rings).

Spacing. To allow for proper drainage and the natural expansion and contraction of the wood, space the lengths of decking slightly apart. Spacers such as 16d nails can help

Proper Fastening

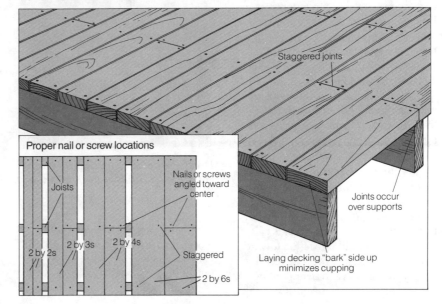

Staggered joints

Proper nail or screw locations

Joists

Nails or screws angled toward center

2 by 2s

2 by 3s

2 by 4s

Staggered

2 by 6s

Joints occur over supports

Laying decking "bark" side up minimizes cupping

you space decking uniformly and quickly. Use two nails, one at each end of the board already secured; set the nails snug against the board and push their tips into the bearing surface. Shove the next board against the nails, then secure it. Yank out the two spacing nails and repeat the process with the remaining boards. For different spacing, use a larger or smaller nail or cut a spacer from wood. Spacing should range from 3/16 to 3/8 inch.

Start by laying one length of decking across the floor joists, beginning at the wall if the deck is house-attached. Align the board parallel to and about 1/8 inch from the house wall. It's fine to let the decking boards run long, since you'll be cutting them off later.

As you fasten decking over the joists, occasionally check the remaining distance to be covered, measuring from both ends of the decking. If you need to adjust the spacing, slightly vary the distance between several pieces to avoid a large adjustment on the last one.

Fastening. Decking can be fastened to joists with nails, screws, special

metal clips, or decking adhesive. Regardless of the method you choose, you may want to screw down decking over water or electrical lines to allow access for repairs.

Fasten the decking boards at every support point (joist or beam). For neater, more professional-looking results, keep visible fasteners in a straight line. If you suspect that your decking is slightly green (not dry), you may wish to use only one nail or screw at each bearing point when you first secure the decking, staggering the fasteners from side to side along the length of the board. This method will allow shrinkage during drying, but will not permit cupping. When the wood has cured—in 6 to 12 months—add a second nail or screw at each bearing point for 2 by 4s or 2 by 6s.

■ *Nails.* The fastest, least expensive way to fasten wooden decking or subflooring to joists or beams is, of course, nailing. Use hot-dipped galvanized common or box nails or, if you're willing to pay a lot more, stainless steel or aluminum alloy nails. Box nails are the easiest to drive through soft woods such as redwood and cedar. Don't use copper or poor-quality galvanized nails, which can discolor the decking. Choose nails long enough to penetrate the joists to a depth at least equal to the decking's thickness.

For a top-quality job, hand-nailing is still favored. It's true that an air-powered nail gun (pneumatic nailer) fastens down decking much more quickly, but the nails it shoots are more inclined to rise up with time; they also tend to sink into the wood a little too far, since redwood, cedar, and some other materials are quite soft.

To keep from splitting boards when nailing, try this carpenter's trick: blunt each nail's tip with a light tap of the hammer, then angle the nails slightly toward the board's center. Nails at board ends should be angled toward adjoining boards; to prevent splitting here, you may have to drill pilot holes three-fourths the diameter of the nail shanks.

As you hammer in each nail, be careful not to crush the wood's surface with the final blows. Stop hammering as soon as the nail is flush with the decking; then, when the deck is completely nailed, set the head of each nail slightly below the surface with a nailset. If you do dent the wood when nailing, splash a little wood sealer on the indentations; the sealer will cause the bruised wood to swell back to its normal size. (If you plan to stain the deck, treat the bruised wood with a rag soaked with warm water; don't use sealer, which may have a tendency to repel the stain.)

As the decking lumber shrinks and swells, the nails will rise slightly. When your deck is about a month old, reset the heads just below the surface, using a hammer and a large nailset.

■ *Screws.* Though they're more expensive than nails, galvanized deck screws (similar to drywall screws) provide secure, high-quality fastening. Screws have several advantages over nails: they don't pop up as readily, their galvanized coating is less likely to be damaged during installation, and they eliminate the problem of hammer dents in the decking. You'll find them

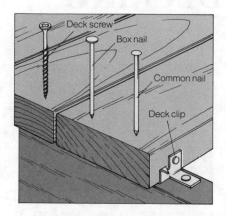

Decking may be fastened with nails, screws, clips, or adhesive (not shown).

surprisingly easy to drive in soft woods such as redwood and cedar if you use an electric drill or screw gun with a Phillips-head screwdriver tip.

Be sure to choose galvanized screws that are long enough to penetrate joists at least as deep as the decking is thick (for 2 by 4 or 2 by 6 decking, buy 3-inch screws). Screws are sold by the pound or, at a substantial savings, by the 25-pound box.

■ *Deck clips.* To eliminate visible fasteners, you can use special deck-fastening clips. Nailed to the sides of decking lumber and secured to joists, these fasteners hide between deck boards. They're far more expensive to buy and more time-consuming to install than nails or screws.

■ *Decking adhesive.* If you want a deck free of visible fasteners, consider installing decking with a special adhesive; you apply it to the joists with a caulking gun, then set the decking boards in place. Keep in mind that the boards will be nearly impossible to remove once the adhesive sets up—a potential problem if you must make repairs later.

Cutting decking. When you're building a deck, a portable circular saw is practically a necessity. Not only does it save agonizing hours of cutting boards to length with a handsaw, but it also allows you to trim off the deck's edges as squarely as any master car-

penter. Just let the decking run at least an inch past the deck's edge lines; once all the boards are nailed down, snap a chalk line carefully along the deck edges and saw along it. Skilled hands can saw freehand along a chalk line; less experienced builders will want to guide the saw with a length of wood tacked to the deck.

Straightening a bowed length of decking. When you're laying decking, you'll find that some boards are too bowed to align properly. To correct the problem, first nail each end of the board to the joists. Then start the nails at their proper locations in the bowed area, over the joists. If the board bows toward an adjoining length of decking, force a chisel between the two and pry the bowed board outward, then nail. If the bow is away from the neighboring board, drive the chisel into the joist at the bow's apex (angle the chisel slightly), then pry the board into place and nail.

Notching for posts or obstacles. If decking must be notched around a post, tree, or other obstacle, hold the decking board in place and mark it for the obstacle. Add ⅛ inch to each side (to allow for drainage), then draw straight lines with a combination

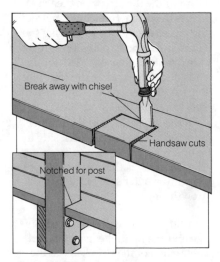

Notch decking to fit around obstacles, using a handsaw and chisel.

square. Cut the sides of the notch with a handsaw, stroking straight up and down; then split out the waste piece with a chisel.

BUILDING A SOLID DECK

Most watertight decking materials are best installed by a professional, such as a mason or roofer. But before these pros can ply their trades, you'll need to build the substructure and (often) cover the joists with plywood. The following information can help you handle these jobs; talk with your contractor about any specific requirements for your deck.

Deck Drainage

Solid-surface decks must be designed with proper rain runoff in mind: the surface must slope toward scuppers

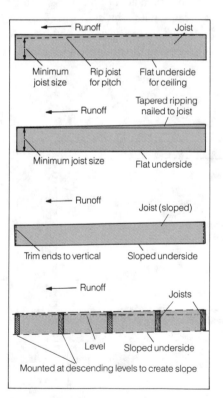

To carry rainwater off deck, joists can be tapered, built up, or installed on a slope.

Installing a Plywood Base

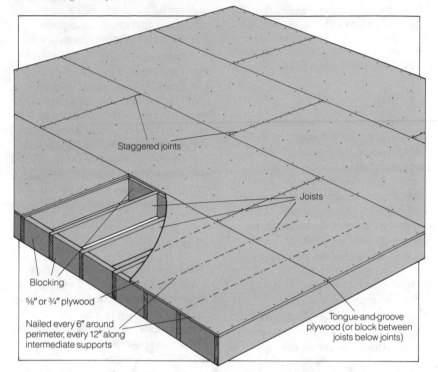

Staggered joints

Joists

Blocking

⅝″ or ¾″ plywood

Nailed every 6″ around perimeter, every 12″ along intermediate supports

Tongue-and-groove plywood (or block between joists below joints)

or gutters that collect the rainwater and carry it away. A typical slope of 1 inch per 10 feet can be created in several ways (see drawing at left).

If joists run in line with the planned runoff, you can rip each one to a taper to create the proper pitch. Because this method leaves the undersides of joists level, it's often the best technique to use if a ceiling will be attached below. If you decide to rip joists in this way, be sure that the narrowest part of the joist won't be less than the minimum joist size (see page 63). Another way to keep the lower edges of joists level is to nail thin, tapered rippings, angled toward the planned runoff, on top of the joists.

Where there won't be a ceiling below, you can simply slope the joists and angle-cut their ends.

If joists run perpendicular to the direction of runoff, you can mount each one about ⅛ inch lower than its neighbor to create the proper slope; the undersides will have to be furred-down if you want to mount a level ceiling below.

Installing a Plywood Base

As a base for watertight decking, nail a solid deck of plywood sheathing to the joists. (For this base type, either choose tongue-and-groove plywood or plan to block between joists.) Stagger ⅝-inch plywood sheets (or ¾-inch sheets for tile or concrete) horizontally across the joists, centering the panel ends on joists. To allow for expansion, leave ⅛ inch between the edges of adjoining panels and ¹⁄₁₆ inch between their ends.

Before installing the plywood, brush the edges of each sheet with a water repellent, primer, or stain. Then nail the plywood at each bearing surface, as shown in the illustration above. To prevent bowing, begin by nailing two adjacent sides, starting from a corner (preferably a corner that butts against other sheets).

When nailing plywood to joists, choose 8d galvanized nails for ⅝-inch and thicker plywood. Space nails every 6 inches along the sides of each panel and every 12 inches at intermediate supports.

LIGHTING, PLUMBING & STORAGE

To make your deck more useful (or simply more enjoyable), consider adding a few special features, such as lighting, plumbing, and trapdoors for access to below-deck storage.

Lighting

Outdoor lighting is a welcome addition to many decks, increasing the daily hours of outdoor use. Have an electrician help you extend your home's 120-volt system to the deck; or, if you prefer, you can install low-voltage lighting fixtures yourself. Home improvement centers and hardware stores may offer low-voltage deck-lighting kits, including post-style lights, transformer, and cable. (For the widest selection of styles, visit a specialty lighting store.)

For a 12-volt system, installation is simple: just plug in the transformer and run the two-wire outdoor cable to fixtures (most transformers can handle several fixtures). Such a system carries far less risk of harmful shock than a 120-volt system does; in fact, in most areas, no electrical permit is required for installing a system extending from a low-voltage plug-in transformer (the most common kind).

Most transformers for outdoor lights are encased in watertight boxes, but it's still wise to install them in a sheltered location at least a foot off the deck or ground. The cable can be laid on the ground or fastened to wooden support members below the decking. Most fixtures connect to cables without requiring you to strip the insulation and splice the wires, and no ground connections are required.

Plumbing

Decks gain comfort and convenience when you pipe water to them. For easy deck maintenance, it's important to provide at least one hose connection; you may also want sprinklers for planters, a shower or outdoor sink, or a fountain, pool, or spa.

Hose bibbs and hoses can be effectively camouflaged in storage boxes recessed below the deck (see bottom of facing page); a 3- by 5-foot chamber makes a handy container for 50 to 100 feet of hose. You can also conceal a hose bibb and hose in a bench with solid sides and a hinged seat, or in a workbench with vertical doors. For other deck storage ideas, see page 43.

Water-piping systems for decks are subject to building code regulations in most areas. If you're short on plumbing experience, plan on getting professional help; if you're handy—and particularly if PVC pipe is allowed by your local codes—you should find installing a couple of hose bibbs an easy job. See the facing page for a typical plumbing configuration.

When to install plumbing. If you have a high-level deck with access to the substructure, you can install pipes after completing your deck. This allows you to live with the new deck long enough to know just where and how you'll want to use water. Putting in an entire system at once costs less than developing it bit by bit.

For low-level decks with limited or no access to the underside, plumbing

Low-Voltage Deck Lighting

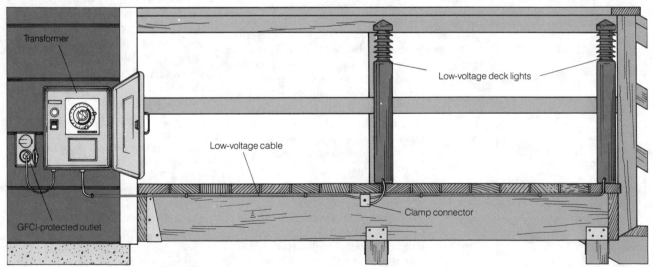

Low-voltage transformer for outdoor lighting system plugs into house receptacle. Two-wire cable is easy to route to any of a variety of deck lighting fixtures. Lay cable on ground or conceal below decking.

must usually be installed before the deck surface is laid—particularly if the pipes must be buried or, where exposed, be insulated or otherwise protected against freezes.

Protecting the pipes. Deck pipes are especially vulnerable to bursting during freezing weather. Main pipes buried beneath the frost line are adequately protected, but short lengths of exposed pipe leading up to faucets should be insulated. If there's extensive piping attached to beams or joists, drain it completely in winter; a good plan is to equip the system with a main cutoff valve inside the house and a drain valve (or threaded plug) at the lowest point in the deck plumbing. During winter, close the main valve and keep the drain valve open (or remove the plug). Also open all faucets or other fixtures and drain any sink traps.

Storage Compartments

There's great potential for outdoor storage right below the surface of most decks. By hinging a section of decking—in essence, making a trapdoor—you'll gain access to a perfect storage area for hoses, outdoor equipment, toys, or even a sandbox.

For any below-deck compartment, construction is similar—and simple. Typical methods are shown in the illustration at right.

Cut the decking for the door so each end rests on the center of a joist or beam. On the door's underside, fasten a 2 by 4 or 2 by 2 parallel to each supporting member to keep the door securely seated. Fasten these strips from beneath with nails or screws that penetrate two-thirds of the way through the decking's thickness. Strap metal secured on a diagonal provides extra support on large doors.

Doors can be set in place and simply lifted out for access, or hinged for greater convenience. If you opt for hinges, use leaf types. To create a finger pull, just drill a hole.

Piping Water to Your Deck

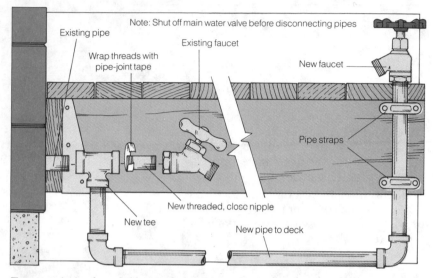

Tap an existing hose bibb simply by adding a plumbing tee to the line.

Deck Storage

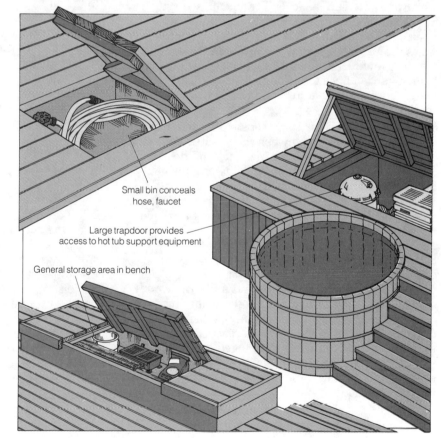

REVIVING AN OLD DECK

It's no wonder a deck begins to show its age after a few years—just consider what it has to endure. Sun beats down on it, turning the wood gray; rain makes it swell and twist; debris fills the cracks between boards; mildew develops under potted plants; and furniture scrapes the decking, feet grind in dirt, and stains besmirch the once-pristine surface.

If you have an existing deck that looks the worse for wear, consider restoring it. You may be surprised at how new you can make it look, even down to the color.

Cleaning Your Deck

Of all the steps involved in restoration, cleaning probably involves the most labor, especially if your deck hasn't been cleaned in a while.

Cleaning between decking. For a healthy deck, maintain maximum air circulation around each board; the debris that builds up between boards slows drainage, keeping wood moist and encouraging the growth of mildew. Use a hard spray of water from a garden hose to dislodge most of the debris, then follow up with a putty knife to knock out any recalcitrant litter.

If your deck's boards are set so close together that a hose can't clean between them, slip an old saw into the cracks and work the blade up and down. Some professionals recommend widening the gap between tightly spaced boards by making a pass with a circular saw with the blade set to match the wood's thickness. (Recommended spacing between boards is 3/16 to 3/8 inch.)

Surface cleaning. Mud tracked over a deck can eventually turn it dusty gray; in shady areas, mold can build up in winter months and make the wood slippery when wet. But the hardest weathering comes from the sun's ultraviolet rays, which break down the wood tissue's lignin—a plasticlike polymer binding the cellulose fibers together. The end product of degraded lignin is simply cellulose in minute strands, and these give boards a tired-looking gray surface.

To remove most of the dirt and old cellulose from your deck, you can scrub it with a solution of trisodium phosphate (TSP) in warm water, using 1 cup of TSP crystals to a gallon of water. Use a stiff brush or a broom with short, stiff bristles, and be sure to wear rubber gloves; if you are scrubbing by hand, wear safety goggles. And if you're going to be on your hands and knees for a while, consider rubber kneepads.

After scrubbing, hose off dirt and excess TSP solution, flushing thoroughly with plain water. If parts of the deck are plagued with mildew, treat them with a solution of 1 part water to 3 parts household bleach. Let stand for a few minutes, then rinse.

Note: Concern about the environmental effects of phosphates is one reason to consider using commercial deck cleaners with active ingredients other than TSP. Such cleaners are more expensive but simpler to use than TSP; they're sold in most home improvement centers. Some of these products contain fungicides and mildewcides; others include special bleaches to lighten the wood.

Power washing. Particularly if you have a large deck, you may want to rent a power washer for the initial cleaning—it will both blast away surface grayness and save you a lot of elbow grease. A power washer delivers about 2,000 pounds per square inch of pressure.

It's a good idea to choose a nozzle with a 25° or 40° spray arc; in the hands of an inexperienced user, a narrower spray can damage the wood. Be sure to wear safety goggles. Work in line with the wood's grain, holding the spray head at a slight angle about 4 to 6 inches above the deck's surface. Move slowly and evenly, overlapping adjacent sprayed areas.

Renewing & Replacing Wood

After the deck is clean and dry, check the condition of the boards, looking for nail stains, splintering, splits, cupping, protruding nail heads, and dry rot. If you have to replace boards, take the time to coat the joists or beams with a wood preservative (see page 94) before nailing on the new wood. Treat new wood with preservative wherever it will be in contact with supporting wood.

Check for rot wherever two pieces of wood meet. If the top edges of joists are rotten, remove any decking you plan to replace and soak the rotted areas with preservative, then nail or screw a treated 2 by 4 or 2 by 6 "partner" onto the side of the rotted member (see drawing on facing page). Rotted posts will need to be replaced; block up the deck for support, then remove the old posts and install new ones made from pressure-treated wood (dip post ends in preservative). If ends of joists are rotted, you can trim them off and soak the raw ends with preservative.

Since wood tends to swell and contract over time, nails can slowly work loose. If you see such rising nails—or any nails that are staining the decking—use a nailset to punch them flush with or slightly below the deck's surface.

Be sure railings and stairs are solid. Rebuild or refasten any problem parts.

Altering Color

Oxalic acid, sold at many paint and hardware stores, can make your just-cleaned deck look almost brand new. It lightens and brightens the wood as you apply it, and it also helps remove nail stains.

Since oxalic acid causes skin irritation, wear rubber gloves and safety goggles when handling it; cover nearby plants, too. Mix 4 ounces of crystals to 1 gallon of warm water. Apply this solution liberally with a sponge, mop, or garden sprayer, but don't use metal buckets, wire brushes, or steel wool. The longer the solution acts on the deck, the more effectively the wood will bleach, so try to work early in the morning or on an overcast day. Before the solution dries, scrub the deck with a stiff bristle broom or brush, then thoroughly hose it off. You'll be left with a deck that looks almost new, but don't expect this color to last; the surface will slowly gray with time.

If you actually prefer the quieter, aged look of an older deck to the brightness of a new one, you can accelerate the graying process by covering the cleaned and scrubbed wood with a solution of 1½ pounds of baking soda and a dash of dish detergent to a gallon of warm water. Mop this on, let it sit, rinse, and repeat.

Adding a Finish

Wood preservatives, clear water repellents, or stains complete the renovation program. These keep the wood from readily absorbing the rainwater that can lead to swelling, cracking, and warping. Wood preservatives contain a higher percentage of fungicides than do most water repellents and stains. (Repellents are sufficient protection for pressure-treated wood.) You'll find more information about wood finishes on page 95.

To apply any finish, brush it on, choosing a cool or cloudy day for the job. Don't work in direct, hot sunlight; you want the finish to soak into the wood, not just evaporate.

Repairing Rotted Substructure

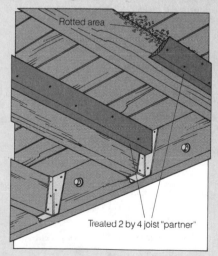

Reinforce rotted top edge of joist by nailing "partner" to side.

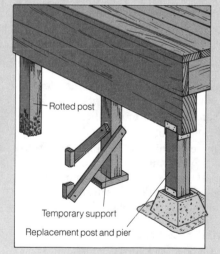

Temporarily support deck before removing and replacing rotted post.

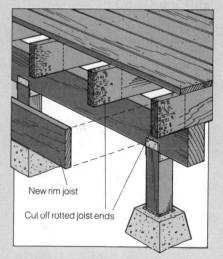

Where joists ends are rotted, you may simply be able to cut them off.

PROTECTING YOUR INVESTMENT

Decay-causing organisms, insects, and weather are the natural enemies of wood, and sooner or later, they'll attack any wooden structure. Fungi and bacteria flourish where humidity or constant exposure to water keeps wood moist or wet; severe weather (especially cold temperatures) can cause checking, splitting, warping, and other related problems. And of course, the surface of your deck takes constant punishment from foot traffic.

To keep your deck looking attractive and add years to its useful life, take care to protect it against moisture and other sources of decay. Your main weapons in the battle will be caulking compounds, preservatives, and wood finishes.

CAULKING COMPOUNDS

Caulking compounds are used during construction to fill exterior cracks or seams that would otherwise let in damaging moisture and invasive insects. These compounds vary in both price and composition, but you'll generally find a direct relationship be-tween cost and quality—cheaper products tend to be less effective than the pricier ones.

For most caulking jobs, the 11-ounce cartridge and the caulking gun (see illustration below left) are simplest to use. The surface to be caulked should be clean, dry, and free from oil. Be sure to check the manufacturer's instructions for any other special requirements. If you plan to paint or stain the surface over the caulking, make sure to choose a "paintable" type.

Elastomeric caulks. These synthetic "supercaulks" are the top of the line. They effectively seal almost any type of crack or joint, they adhere to most materials, and they will outlast ordinary caulks by many years. Look for the generic types of elastomeric caulks, including polysulfides, polyurethanes, and silicones.

Besides their higher price, these products do have a few other drawbacks. Silicone rubber is awkward to smooth out once applied, and it doesn't accept paint; polysulfides can't be used on porous surfaces unless a special primer is applied first.

Latex, acrylic latex, and butyl-rubber caulks. Several medium-priced, all-purpose caulks offer average performance. Among them are latex, acrylic latex, and butyl-rubber caulks.

Latex and acrylic latex types vary in price and quality. Acrylic latex caulks outperform nonacrylic latexes, but both are easy to apply, and you can clean your tools with water.

Butyl-rubber caulk is generally more flexible and durable than acrylic latexes; it can be used on any type of surface or material. Keep in mind, however, that it tends to shrink slightly while curing.

Oil-based caulks. These are the lowest priced, lowest performance caulks on the market. They're not recommended for exterior use.

WOOD PRESERVATIVES

Though you can apply wood preservatives yourself, the most effective method of application is pressure treatment at a mill; this process forces chemical preservatives deep into the wood fibers. Pressure-treated species such as Southern pine or Douglas fir are as durable as the hardier types like redwood, cedar, and cypress heartwoods. The preservatives used may not affect a wood's appearance at all, but some do leave a discoloration that must be covered with paint or stain.

When buying pressure-treated wood, look for a quality mark from the American Wood Preservers Bureau (AWPB); it's your guarantee that the treatment meets established standards. The AWPB mark also gives you information about the wood's proper use: depending on the amount of chemical injected, the wood may be labeled "22, ground-contact use" or "L.P. 2, above-ground use." For more about pressure-treated woods, turn to page 51.

To apply preservatives to untreated wood, you can use a brush or simply immerse the lumber in a large bucket, drum, or makeshift trough (use two lumber stacks with polyethylene sheeting draped between them, as illustrated on the facing page). The long-term results of do-it-yourself application are less satisfactory than factory treatment, though.

If you do plan to apply preservatives, ask your building-supply dealer to recommend products that are both effective and safe to use. Several once-popular preservatives, including pentachlorophenol, creosote, and arsenic compounds, have been banned from consumer sales because of health risks, and additional chemicals may be added to the list.

Copper naphthenate is one relatively safe and effective preservative you can brush onto lumber. Because it's nontoxic to plants and animals, it's

Caulking Gun

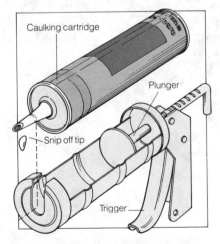

Caulking cartridge

Plunger

Snip off tip

Trigger

Caulking gun holds cartridge of caulking compound or adhesive.

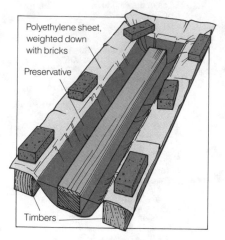

Make a trough from lumber and polyethylene for soaking lumber in preservatives.

especially useful for treating garden structures. The dark green tinge it leaves on treated wood can be covered with two coats of paint.

Note: When applying any preservative, wear rubber gloves and follow the manufacturer's directions.

WOOD FINISHES

As discussed on page 50, species and grades of wood vary in their resistance to natural damage. Some types are decay resistant by nature, and pressure-treated woods have just as great a resistance. But because no wood is completely impervious to damaging environmental effects, all types benefit from a finish to guard against weathering, accidental staining, and decay. Finishes change a wood's color or tone, and may mask its grain or texture. Possible choices include clear water repellents, stains, and paints; bleach—more a cosmetic treatment than a finish—is discussed under "Altering Color," page 93.

Note: Remember that finishes are not always essential. The most natural-looking decks are often left to weather naturally; redwood, for example, will turn a silvery gray after a year or two. The right degree of protection and finish for your deck depends on the climate, grade and species of wood, and the look you want to achieve.

Clear water repellent, also known as water sealer, protects wood and helps prolong its beauty. It doesn't color wood (unless you buy a pigmented type), but does darken it slightly. You can apply a penetrating water repellent before staining, but if you do this, you'll generally have to wait a few months after the sealer's application before adding the stain.

Water repellent may also be applied over a stain to provide additional protection, though many stains already contain such a repellent.

Stains come in two color intensities. Semitransparent types contain enough pigment to tint the wood surface, but not enough to hide the natural grain. Solid color stains contain more pigment; many of them are almost as opaque as paint, making them excellent choices for masking lower grades of lumber.

Stains come in a variety of colors, from pale gray through the darkest wood colors; it's also possible to devise custom tints by adding paint pigments to stains. Be sure to choose "nonchalking" stains to keep foot traffic from carrying residue into your house. If you're staining pressure-treated wood, take care to choose a stain made just for that purpose.

Paint chips or brochures can only indicate a stain's typical appearance. To see how a particular product will actually look on your deck, you'll need to apply it to a scrap piece of your decking lumber.

Heavy-bodied stains may be brushed, rolled, or sprayed on. Light-bodied types are rolled or sprayed on, then brushed smooth; they can also be applied in two coats, using a brush only. Stains generally require reapplication every 2 or 3 years.

Deck paints, in opaque colors from muted to vibrant, successfully mask defects in lower grades of lumber. On the down side, they're harder to apply and maintain than stains; to keep your deck looking good, you may have to repaint it nearly every year. Moreover, once it's painted, a deck can only be repainted—never finished naturally or stained.

Be sure the paint you buy is suitable for a deck. One popular choice is quick-drying, self-priming alkyd-based deck paint. Marine enamels, though they last a long time, are quite expensive.

For the most enduring painted finish, pretreat the lumber with water repellent before you build the deck. If you'll be applying a primer, do it after the substructure is up but before laying the decking; wait to put on the primer until a few days after applying the repellent. Apply top coats after the deck is completed.

Pay special attention to the chemical compatibility of the water repellent, primer, and top coat. Be sure that the manufacturer's recommendations apply specifically to the treatment and finish you're using, and that these materials are suitable for decks. Using materials that all come from the same manufacturer will give you a head start on compatibility, but even in this case, check the labels to be sure.

Try to paint on a cool, windless day. Paint often dries so quickly in hot weather that it fails to bond properly—and if conditions are dusty as well as hot, the deck's surface may be marred or roughened. If you must paint on a hot, dry day, work only after the sun is low so the paint will dry slowly.

Before painting, always sweep or dust surfaces. Also make sure the wood is dry; if it's moist, the paint may fail to adhere, leading to blistering or other failure. Apply paint with either a brush or roller.

INDEX